Praise for *Lessons From the Edge*

'My dear friend Aldo has travelled across the world on his many other adventures with many friends; I've had the privilege to travel one of the toughest environments on earth with him. We shared a lot of laughter. I'd definitely say when the chips are down you want Aldo on your side. An inspiring read from a top bloke and good mate.'
– Tom Hardy

'Aldo has had my back for over 20 years, from the Royal Marines to anti-poaching patrols, rowing the Atlantic together and dodging narcos. If you want an epic book of unbelievable tales, then this is it.'
– Jason Fox

'From young Scout, to Commando sniper and on to a life of high expedition adventure. Aldo's story is both inspiring and humbling.'
– Bear Grylls

'Aldo Kane is a real-life Action Man. This book is a must read for those that want to thrive in these uncertain times.'
– Jamie Redknapp

'Aldo has been tested under enemy fire and by cartel crazies, under lethal rockfall, exploding volcanoes and in stuttering helicopters. He never loses his cool or makes the wrong call, always carries the biggest load and takes the worst sleeping spot. He is the first name on every *Expedition* team's wishlist.'
– Steve Backshall

For Anna & Atlas
— To the ends of the Earth

LESSONS FROM THE EDGE

INSPIRATIONAL TALES OF SURVIVING, THRIVING AND EXTREME ADVENTURE

ALDO KANE

First published in Great Britain in 2021 by Yellow Kite
An imprint of Hodder & Stoughton
An Hachette UK company

1

Copyright © Aldo Kane 2021

Co-writer: Ben Dirs

Picture research by Jane Smith Media

A CIP catalogue record for this title is available from the British Library

Hardback ISBN 978 1 529 35072 2
eBook ISBN 978 1 529 35073 9

Typeset in Bembo by Hewer Text UK Ltd, Edinburgh
Printed and bound in Great Britain by Clays Ltd, Elcograf S.p.A.

Hodder & Stoughton policy is to use papers that are natural, renewable
and recyclable products and made from wood grown in sustainable forests.
The logging and manufacturing processes are expected to conform
to the environmental regulations of the country of origin.

Yellow Kite
Hodder & Stoughton Ltd
Carmelite House
50 Victoria Embankment
London EC4Y 0DZ

www.yellowkitebooks.co.uk

Contents

PROLOGUE

Iraq 2003

My partner and I watch silently. We are the sniper team, the eyes and ears of the unit. The rest of the company advance steadily through the scrubby land in front of us. I see friendly faces through my scope as I scan the distant tree line for enemy positions, dismissing all distractions to focus on the job in hand. I search the date palm plantation and buildings dotted among the trees, then the ground ahead of the advancing men, then the treeline again. A small movement catches my eye. I'm drawn to a rooftop well over 500 metres away.

Through the scope I see three men moving hurriedly around on the flat roof – in the direction we're advancing on, and from where we had just been ambushed, RPGs (rocket-propelled grenades) sent whistling over our heads and exploding all around us. I give a target indication to the boss over my radio. This is where the sniper role comes into its own. 'Take the shot,' is the command.

Years of training have prepared me for this moment. My spotter goes through the process we have practised so many times: I make the required adjustments. My partner confirms I understand everything. Then I wait . . .

The final step is: Time to fire. My mind is empty and every breath I take is controlled. I feel incredibly aware. Of the wind, or lack of it. Of the temperature. So, so hot. Of the weight of my rifle.

As I take up first pressure on the trigger, I see my mate Shiner and other troops still moving towards the enemy, unaware of the shooters. Second pressure – the shot is released and an irreversible chain reaction has begun. I'm almost surprised, because I'm in such a calm state of concentration.

The heat haze vortexes in the wake of the speeding bullet, as if in slow-motion high definition. The single ultrasonic crack whips in front of the advancing troops and alerts them to the direction of the enemy. This is the job I am here to do, have been trained to do – which is what makes pulling the trigger so simple. And yet it's far from simple.

When I took the shot that day, two lives changed.

2017, Democratic Republic of the Congo

Fourteen years have passed and I'm in Mount Nyiragongo, an active – and angry – volcano, the most dangerous in Africa. And when I say I'm 'in' the volcano, I mean that literally – I'm 500 metres down inside the volcano crater. I've been this far down before, and tried and failed twice to make it to the bottom of the crater, but this time the conditions seem perfect. No excuses.

It is the most surreal experience – spectacular but daunting. Around and above me is the jaw-dropping amphitheatre of the volcano's crater, about one kilometre wide. Crumbling and broken ledges left over from previous eruptions line the perilous inner walls as I navigate my way down through the lowest unstable layers, towards the lava lake at the bottom – the largest and most violent lava lake in the world.

Getting that deep requires hours of different rope techniques, abseils and traverses down and across the crumbling rock, searching for secure areas and hoping to avoid the constant rockslides, including boulders that would take my head off. The noise of huge crashing rocks fills the air and, coupled with the overpowering smell of sulphur and the ferocious bubbling and whooshing heat from below, makes it clear that I am truly inside the very hydraulics of the planet.

There is a last 80-metre drop to the crater floor, and I check with those watching from above before starting the descent. My mouth is dry, I'm sweating profusely. I am acutely aware that if anything goes wrong, there is no rescue. I am on my own. Every tiny decision matters in this moment.

Landing on the base of the crater, achievement that it is, doesn't lessen the adrenaline or anxiety. Beneath the boulder I'm standing on is a thick stream of black solidified lava. I've talked myself into believing it's a dangerous place to be for a very good reason: because it is. I come off the ropes, do a short piece to the camera on my phone and assess the situation. A mere 70 metres in one direction is the furious lava lake. About 60 metres in another direction is a mini-volcano which erupted and almost killed me the last time I attempted to reach this spot. I have this overwhelming feeling of insignificance, of being out of place, somewhere humans have no business being.

Time to bow out. I don't want to push my luck. If anyone knows how tenuous life is, it's me.

Going inside that volcano was just part of the plan I made after pulling that trigger. In truth, I'd been pushing myself and making big, extreme life choices since I was a kid. And Commando training taught me that getting to where you want to be in life, both personally and professionally, takes hard work, time and a plan. But it was my time in Iraq, and the terrible truths of war, that showed me just how fragile life really is. It made everything seem so much more urgent.

So what do I want to show you, the reader? I want you to realise that life might be bigger than you think. I want you to believe that you are capable of great things. Because if a non-academic kid from an estate in Kilwinning, a kid soldier who hit the skids and lost direction, managed to turn it around so spectacularly, then so can you.

Before embarking on my dream job – travelling to every corner of the earth, leading movie stars into active volcanoes and so much more – this apparently tough military man had to cope with feeling suddenly worthless aged 26, having left the Marines and everything I knew. Doors literally slammed in my face.

How did I come to realise that you can't wait for things to happen? How did I find purpose and belonging? Well, stick with me and I'll tell you how. I've never shared these adventures and lessons before, at least not in this much detail. And writing it all down has made me realise just how colourful and instructive it's been. The ups *and* the downs, the whole lot. I hope you can take inspiration from my experiences.

A few weeks ago, I watched the birth of my son, Atlas, via a high-speed internet link from the middle of the Atlantic Ocean. Becoming a father has given me a new perspective on life and is the start of a whole new mysterious adventure. Deploying on extreme, remote and hostile missions had always been my bread and butter, but it was more than just a way of making a living. It was also a way of challenging myself, physically and mentally. I can only hope that the mission of fatherhood will be filled with challenges and learning experiences every bit as big. This is what drives me onwards.

Adventure is my lifeblood – take it away and I am no longer me. I travel to explore the extremes of our world and my own head. I see our natural world as a teaching ground, somewhere I can hone my abilities and push myself to the limit. However, what I've learned out there on the edge are the skills we all need to survive on this planet, whether you're trying to escape from an angry polar bear or negotiate a tricky situation in your office job.

Maybe you don't want to be a television field producer, surrounded by Ebola in Africa, or abseil into volcanoes or row across the Atlantic. But do you want to be robust enough, physically and mentally, to handle whatever life throws at you? Do you want the fortitude to do what you're afraid of? Do you want to nail those goals you've been scared to tackle? Do you want to learn that failure isn't necessarily the end and can be your very own turning point?

You only get one crack at life, and the impossible is possible. Don't believe me?

Then read on.

CHAPTER 1

Earning the Right: Courage, Determination, Unselfishness and Cheerfulness in the Face of Adversity

How do you end up hanging out in volcanoes for a living? Or hunting tiger traffickers? Or trying to reason with drug dealers who are out of their minds and pointing guns at your head? This is the sort of stuff careers advisors aren't likely to mention. For me at least, not having much choice probably helped.

Had I been academic in the traditional sense, maybe I'd have ended up in an office the whole of my working life, wondering why I was angry and dying inside. Had I grown up richer, at least financially, maybe that would have been my future. But when you're a working-class kid from an ordinary town in Scotland, not much is really expected of you. And it's often people who aren't predicted to achieve much who lead the most extraordinary lives. When almost everyone assumes you're unexceptional, you can go out on a few limbs, without the risk of letting anyone down. Including yourself.

I was born and raised in East Kilbride, on the outskirts of Glasgow. East Kilbride is a typical new town, with lots of concrete – housing estates, shopping centres, dual carriageways and roundabouts. It's full of respectable, working-class folk and a sound enough place. But the fact I lived there for the first decade of my life and can't remember much about it tells its own story.

Mum and Dad got married at 21 and had five children under the age of six by the time they were 28. First to arrive were me and my twin Ross, followed by my sister Stroma and younger brothers Struan and Ruairidh. Good Gaelic names, chosen while Mum and Dad were cycling around Scotland on their honeymoon.

Dad was an ambulance technician and Mum was a housewife until all five of us were at school, when she trained as a midwife. Later, she became a paramedic and worked with my dad. It scares me now, thinking about raising five kids on one income. And not a big income at that. That's a lot of hungry mouths to feed, but I never felt deprived. Not having much money was normal. My mum knitting jumpers for me was normal. I'm not sure twins wearing matching knitted jumpers was normal – Ross and I had AK and RK on the front of ours – but at least they showed how much our mum cared.

When I was 11, we moved about 30 miles, to Kilwinning in Ayrshire. That's really when you can start connecting the dots. Ayrshire had its affluent areas, but parts of it were pretty rough. Because it was on the west coast of Scotland, close to Northern Ireland, there was a lot of sectarian violence, Catholic versus Protestant, and beatings and stabbings were fairly common. But because Dad was a Scout leader, Ross and I were involved in Scouting well below the normal age, which kept us out of trouble. Dad had also been a Cub and an Explorer Scout, and I remember him going off to walk the West Highland Way on his own when we were too small to join in. In addition, my sister was one of the first female Scouts in Scotland.

The Scouts have struggled in terms of public perception, and there was a time when you only had to mention the Scouts and someone would call you a geek. But I've got a lot to thank the Scouting movement for. Instead of roaming the streets, drinking and smoking, Ross and I were off on Scout hikes and camps from as young as I can remember, out in the wild, learning to build fires and 'survive'.

The Scouts could be described as a natural training ground for the military. It was, after all, founded by Robert Baden-Powell, who was a decorated officer at the height of the British Empire. I loved the fieldcraft, living off the land, and doing things most people tell themselves they don't want to do: yomping for miles, climbing things, slumming it, being at the mercy of the elements. I always felt super-connected to nature in a way that most kids nowadays aren't. I'd ask myself questions like: How would I eat if there wasn't a shop down the road? How would I stay warm and dry if I got lost in the middle of nowhere? I was taught about resourcefulness, improvisation and overcoming problems on the camps or jamborees. You'd be in your team of six and be judged on campcraft, cleanliness and ingenuity – for example, making a shoe rack for your boots or somewhere to hang wet clothes would earn you extra points. And you'd use your knife to make all of these things. I had a knife from when I was four or five, and I kept it with me always as it was such a useful tool. In the Scouts we'd say, 'Carry a knife, save a life.'

Even when we weren't officially Scouting, we'd be Scouting. Mum and Dad would drive us all up to Glencoe, in the Scottish Highlands, where Dad had gone as a boy with his sister and parents. All seven of us would be squeezed into our long, black Austin Princess hearse (I'd be mortified when they picked me up from school in it, but it did the job until they traded it for a VW camper). We'd park it up, set up camp by the side of the River Coe and head out for a long hike in the Hidden Valley. After dinner, Dad would make us do the hike again in the dark.

9

It sounds a bit mad – and dangerous – but those night hikes were the best. And an education. Walking at night gives you a whole new perspective on the land and the way you move, because noise travels further at night. I was fascinated by the world after dark, when most people are indoors. Later, on military operations, darkness would be a comforting cloak.

Dad didn't know it, but he was planting seeds in our heads. When we were barely out of primary school, Ross and I would often go walking three or four hours from home. We spent more and more time sleeping outside, making fires, catching fish, foraging and making shelters. It sounds like a childhood from Victorian times, but this was the late 1980s.

Another fortunate thing about the great outdoors is that it costs you nothing. My siblings and I didn't have the latest trainers, or computers or TVs in our bedrooms, so we were very good at making our own fun. That's why not having much money was never really important to me, because it didn't translate into an unhappy childhood. We might have got a few comments about the state of our rucksacks or boots on Scout hikes, but we could live with that.

I was also fascinated about how things worked, how they were created and how A got to B. When I was 11, I wrote a letter to the Kelvingrove Museum in Glasgow to ask how taxidermy was done. They invited me in and showed me their fridges full of deer, big cats and bears, and explained the techniques involved. After that, I started collecting dead animals. I'd bury them in the garden, before digging them up later and storing them in shoe boxes under my bed. In case you were wondering – yes, they stank. My first attempt at taxidermy was on a bird, which involved me opening it up, stuffing it with cotton wool and wiring its bones. That poor bird is not currently on display at Kelvingrove Museum.

As my wife points out, this sounds like something a serial killer might do as a child. But being outside a lot meant that we saw plenty of dead animals and I was curious about the mechanics of death – how something could be fully functioning one second and expired the next; the complexity and vulnerability of life. I have a curious mind and like to understand things. As a result, I can be infuriatingly logical. For most of my childhood, we didn't have a TV in the house. But when we did get one, no one would watch films with me because I wouldn't stop asking questions: 'Why would he do that? Would that really happen? Absolutely no chance ...'

I wasn't interested in school because I couldn't see it leading anywhere. I didn't get bad grades in maths because I was stupid, I just couldn't understand the point of being good at it, so never put in the effort. From an early age, I could see through the age-old paradigm of getting an education, followed by a job, followed by working yourself to death while being unhappy. I understood why so many smart kids fell through the cracks – because they didn't fit the narrow definition of 'intelligent'. To me, it was clear life was more about making a plan and acquiring the skills and doing the graft to be able to carry out that plan. I'd already learned far more outside the classroom than inside and I felt that anyone could do anything if they truly worked at it. I was vocational and knew that my education wasn't going to take place in a classroom, learning by rote. I was being taught by teachers who had never travelled, never put everything on the line or taken any risks. I guess much of my work ethic came from my parents. My father is a caring, loving man who showed me the value of working hard, making the most of nature and being able to make things from scratch with my own hands.

I was bullied at school for not being into sport, or at least the games most kids thought were acceptable. Which basically meant football. Running was something I was good at, but running wasn't seen as cool. And orienteering was something nerds did. I also didn't have the 'proper' gear, like the latest trainers. As a result, I'd get roughed up by the so-called hard kids. I guess you could say I was different. When you're at school, all most kids want to do is fit in. But I never understood why you'd want to be the same as everyone else. That was another great thing about the Scouts – it attracted the kids who had passion and the courage not to follow the crowd.

When we were 12, Ross and I joined the Air Cadets – 1138 Squadron in Ardrossan, a few miles from home on the coast. The Scouts had provided the perfect grounding, but we needed a bigger challenge by then. We wanted to be fully self-sufficient, not just surviving in the great outdoors, but thriving. And it didn't take me long to work out that I wanted to join the Royal Marines, the UK's Commando Force.

On our first Cadets camp up in RAF Kinloss in the Highlands, we were immersed in military camp life for 10 days. I don't recall much about the training camp other than one event, which would change the course of my life. I was in the NAAFI shop buying sweets when a man swaggered to the front of the queue, just in front of me. He was wearing a military flying suit, but he walked differently from the other pilots I'd seen – with an air of easy confidence. Before he paid for his items, he put his beret on the counter. To this day, I can picture it – it was a green beret, with a black badge on the front that looked like a globe. I asked him what it was and reached out to touch it. I must have looked like Gollum, utterly transfixed. Except I was overwhelmed by the need to have that beret, rather than a ring.

The man looked at me and said, '*That* is a Green Beret. I'm a Royal Marines Commando helicopter pilot. And you can't touch it, you have to earn it.' Then he walked away.

I promised myself right then that one day I would earn my own Green Beret.

From that point on, I knew I was going to try to become a Marine at the earliest opportunity. Most kids don't know what they want to do after they've left school, but I was consumed by a single goal when I was barely a teenager. I was going to be a Royal Marine – an elite soldier, the best of the best, a Commando specialist spearheading any conflict zone around the world.

You'd think adults would love the fact that I had an ambition, but that wasn't the case. When a careers advisor asked me what I wanted to do when I left school, I told him I was joining the Marines. He didn't look convinced. When he asked what I wanted to do for work experience, I told him I'd like to do something in the outdoors, maybe be a ghillie (a hunting attendant) on an estate. Instead, I ended up in a menswear shop in Irvine, folding shirts and jeans.

By the age of 13, Ross and I were spending all our school holidays on training camps. At 14, we were flying Chipmunks and Bulldogs – tandem aircraft with a trainer in the front and us in the back. Then we found ourselves in the armed forces careers office at 78 Queen Street, Glasgow. When we looked through the brochures – for the RAF, the Parachute Regiment and the Royal Marines – the Marines looked cooler than the rest. Their brochure was all about being on ships and fighting in the jungle and the desert. I even loved their motto: *Per Mare Per Terram* (By Sea By Land). It suggested beach raids and cliff assaults, all that classic Commando stuff. Having to kill anyone didn't enter my head. It just looked like the 'Boy's Own' adventures I'd been reading about in comics like *Commando* since I was small. Marines training was also meant to be the hardest in the world, which appealed to me. I didn't just want to be a soldier, I wanted to be one of the very best soldiers.

Ross and I became regular visitors to 78 Queen Street. The officers knew we were too young but didn't discourage us. They'd tell us to jump on a bar and do 10 pull-ups. The first time we could only do two or three, which was embarrassing. But when they told us to get training, we did.

Gyms weren't a thing when I was a kid. As you'd expect, most of the graft took place outdoors instead. On Fridays after school, Ross and I would get the train to Ardrossan, which took about an hour, then catch the ferry over to Arran. We'd spend the next 48 hours yomping all over the island, with packs on our backs. We'd think nothing of doing 70-odd miles, including up and over the highest mountain on Arran, Goatfell, which is almost a 900-metre ascent. All that training was a means to an end – getting stronger legs and being able to carry a lot of weight over tough terrain – the end, of course, being to obtain the coveted Green Beret of the Royal Marine Commandos.

When Ross and I were 15 years and nine months old – as early as we could – we took a day off school, went for an interview at the careers office and signed the relevant paperwork. We couldn't start the training process until we were 16, but we were champing at the bit. We figured that if we didn't get through the selection process, we'd simply keep trying until we did.

Mum and Dad had to give their permission, and they weren't exactly over the moon. There were a few conversations along the lines of, 'Maybe you need to wait until you're older', or

'Have you thought about the Air Force?' I understood their concern, but my mind had been made up for years by then.

Looking back, my obsession with joining the Marines had a lot to do with my circumstances, rather than some pre-ordained sense of destiny. The truth was, I came from an area that wasn't exactly brimming with opportunities. Unless you were looking to work in a factory, like the majority of school leavers. We felt quite isolated in Kilwinning, which is a 45-minute train ride from Glasgow. That's why four or five of my mates joined the Navy or Air Force and one joined the Paras. They were thinking, 'Let's get the hell out of here sooner rather than later and see what else is out there.'

First up was the Potential Recruits Course (PRC) at Commando Training Centre Royal Marines (CTCRM) in Lympstone, Devon. Ross and I were picked up in Glasgow and driven down on a bus. On arrival, there were a couple of lectures about what it's like to be in the Marines, emphasising that we were attempting to join one of the world's most elite fighting forces, before the hard work began. For three days, me, Ross and about 50 other hopefuls – mainly aged between 22 and 26 – were put through the wringer. There were log carries, endurance courses and Tarzan assault courses – designed to 'sort the wheat from the chaff'. It didn't help that I was quite badly injured – with bad shin splints and a spiral stress fracture down my leg – but I managed to pass, as did Ross.

I look at 16-year-olds now and think, 'I don't know how I did what I did back then.' But when you're a kid, you don't think about things as deeply. My attitude was, 'Right, make sure you don't get injured *too* badly or fuck it up and this is what you could be doing for a job.' It was that simple. Of the 50 or so hopefuls who started, only eight of us got through to the next stage – Basic Training.

On the bus back up to Glasgow, Ross and I got properly pissed for the first time. That was a heady day. I had my GCSEs coming up, but knew I wasn't going to bother sitting most of them. Our join-up date for Basic Training was 5 September and all we needed to get into the Marines were Maths and English, so that's all I was going to bother with. As our joining day got closer, though, Ross started to have a bit of a wobble. He suddenly thought he might want to stay on at school and do A levels.

We'd been planning this adventure together for years and then a couple of days before we were due to head down to Lympstone, and after I'd almost finished packing, he finally announced he wasn't coming. In truth, it didn't have anything to do with wanting to sit his A levels, he'd actually met a girl and fallen madly in love. She'd later become his wife.

Ross was my twin brother. We had shared a bedroom for 16 years. We'd trekked hundreds of miles and camped out under the stars for countless nights together. We'd shared the same dream of joining the Marines and been through so much pain to pass the PRC. We were meant to be one of the first sets of twins to go through training in the same troop. And he'd bailed on me. In truth, I've always looked up to Ross, as much now as I did back then. He was always the best at everything we did, while I muddled through. He was also my wingman, so I was gutted he wasn't coming with me.

Striking out on my own was not what I'd planned but, unsettled as I was, there was no way I was backing out. I knew it was my calling, and there had also been a lot of paperwork involved. So, on the morning of 5 September 1994, I set off from Kilwinning station while my whole family stood on the platform and waved goodbye. Including Ross. For the first time in my life, I was well and truly on my own. Looking back, that was a pivotal moment. I was like a stone being released down a hill. It felt like something big was finally happening to me.

Getting off the train at Lympstone Commando station, I was excited. Just the fact that the station was exclusively for Marines made me feel special. That feeling didn't last long. I'd been on the platform a matter of seconds when a corporal marched over and roared in my face, 'What's your name?'

'Aldo Kane,' I replied.

He bellowed back, 'It's not Aldo-fucking-anything! I'm not your fucking dad! You are Recruit Kane ...!'

Between yells, he cracked me in the nuts with his pace stick – the wooden drill instrument used for measuring the perfect step length. That was my introduction to 30 weeks of what most people would think of as hell – the hardest infantry training, physically and mentally, a recruit can do, probably anywhere in the world.

There were only two or three 16-year-olds in the 50 who started the course. Almost all the rest were fully fledged men, 20 and over. But I reckon my age gave me an advantage. If you join at 24, say, you might have a partner and a kid. You've probably had a job that paid you a lot more than the Marines are going to pay you. That makes it a lot easier to chuck it all in when things get tough. I'd been working for years – from the age of 12 I'd do a paper round before school. Then, when I was 14, I'd get up at 3am and deliver milk until 7, then do the paper round until 8 then on to school – no wonder I had trouble concentrating. But I didn't know what it was to earn a proper wage and have grown-up responsibilities. I only knew what was right in front of me.

For seven months, I was yelled at and worked from the second I opened my eyes in the morning to the moment I was allowed to collapse into bed at night. It got to the point where I could hear the shouting in my dreams. It was obviously tough physically, but becoming a Royal Marine isn't just about running for miles with loads of kit on. Yes, you do a lot of running, but half of almost every day is learning in the classroom: the basics of soldiering and infantry, defence, ambushes and the principles of marksmanship. All the cool stuff I'd been reading about for years.

Royal Marine recruits are nicknamed 'nods', because they're always nodding off during lectures. We would sit with sharpened pencils under our chins, so that if we did nod off, we'd be stabbed awake again. But if they did catch us falling asleep, they'd make us stand up. And if they caught us falling asleep while we were standing up, we'd be chucked out of the class. And I don't mean out of the door, I mean they'd open the window, push us out and make us hang on to the windowsill. Sometimes, the classroom would be a couple of storeys up, which is why they called it 'fruit bats'.

Luckily, it wasn't actually school. Basic training was learning about stuff I'd been thinking about for years, things I was actually interested in – like survival, close quarter combat, weapon handling, live firing exercises and hard physical training. So many times, I found myself thinking, 'Bloody hell, I'm here. I'm actually doing it! And it's just as exciting as I thought it would be.' I've always been able to capture the moment, step outside my body and picture myself in the scene.

I quickly realised the officers and training team were not my mates. There was a lot of being shouted at. And every time I made a mistake, I'd get hammered. Because I was so young, every day they made me stand and drink a pint of milk in front of the entire troop. Sometimes I'd get an extra punishment because they knew Ross was supposed to be on the course with me. While I was crawling through gorse bushes, they'd shout, 'Do it again! That's for your twin who didn't turn up! So that he can feel it, too!'

I knew from the bollockings Mum and Dad had given me that words couldn't harm me. My parents weren't particularly strict, but we pushed the limits like a lot of kids. There was the time Dad caught me paralytic drunk (thankfully, he only found one empty bottle of lager and thought that's all I'd drunk). Even that telling-off – and it was a big one – washed right over me. Ross was different, he'd sulk for two or three days after a bawling out. But I instinctively felt able to rationalise being shouted at. I understood it was just a process, what they had to do – that it wasn't personal. So I never felt like I was being bullied during training. Our ability to get through things was being judged, end of story. I'm not sure where this ability to separate myself from my circumstances came from, but I was able to focus on what I was trying to achieve, while understanding that I was the one person who could ensure that I made it to the end of the course. I was in control of the outcome.

I wasn't actually really good at anything – not the strongest or the fastest or the best at marksmanship. I wasn't even particularly fit compared to some of the older guys. I was and still am distinctly average at most things, but I knew that giving 100% to everything consistently would ensure success. I never got complacent. For the whole seven months, I felt like I was on the verge of messing up and throwing it all away. That kept me sharp and held me accountable.

Everyone on that course was physically fit enough to pass, but not everyone was mentally strong enough. Some of the fittest and strongest people on the course left because they couldn't keep at it all of the time. And a major part of that was being able to put up with bullshit. Self-discipline matters in the military; it finds people out. If you're not able to deal with all the stuff they throw at you in training, you're never going to be able to do the actual job when things get tough. They know that and you learn it.

The pressure is not just about building character, it's also about teaching that one small mistake, one tiny piece of indiscipline, can have catastrophic results. That's why if someone's button is undone in training, everyone is punished for it. You might ask, 'What does it matter if someone's button is undone in training?' It's because in the real world of soldiering, an undone button might be an ammunition box lid not fastened shut or a piece of kit left behind. Which might lead to something else.

In the Marines, they say that a single button left undone can mean 200 soldiers being killed, and a phrase we use if someone sees a button undone is 'submarine hatch' – the button eventually leads to bigger mistakes like leaving a hatch open and killing people. So the harassment and stress and adversity are also about weeding out untrustworthy recruits, those who might not have your back in battle or a 'lack of minerals'. It doesn't matter if they're good blokes and can do all the physical stuff standing on their heads, it's more complex than that. It's also part of why the Royal Marines are known as the 'thinking man's soldier', with over 60% of the 'Gravs' being degree-educated (Gravs is slang for bottom-rung Marines, deriving from 'gravel belly').

Every few weeks, they'd really crank up the bullshit when they wanted to get rid of some dead wood. We'd finish a full day's training, maybe involving being worked for hours on Woodbury Common, then come back for lectures. We'd have dinner, and then they'd take us out for another endurance test on the estuary. We'd look like a load of giant fish who'd missed the tide, all thrashing around in the mud. They'd keep us running and crawling around in that mud for two or three hours – the infamous Marine mud runs – during which time people would be sticking their hands up and saying, 'Fuck this! I don't need it. I'm out!'

But I knew I couldn't be kicked off the course for being shit at crawling around in the mud, and that as long as I didn't put my hand up, I'd live to fight another day.

There was one time I came close to walking away though. We'd all been on a three-hour mud run and all of us were black from head to toe, when someone suddenly announced that we had six minutes to get changed into Introduction to Military Fitness (IMF) kit – pristine white shorts, pristine green rugby jersey and pristine white trainers. Obviously, that's unachievable – there are 30 lads covered in mud and only six showers between us. You know it, they know it. That's the point.

When no one was outside after the six minutes were up, the training corporal shouted, 'Right, you didn't do that. Get back down to the bottom field.' And we all had to do another mud run in our IMF kit.

By the time we got back in again, it was pushing 9pm. Then another corporal bellowed, 'Right, you've got six minutes to get into your drill kit and be in the drill shed . . .'

Again, they knew that was unachievable. When we were late to the drill shed, they ordered us back to our accommodation, where they told us we had until eight the following morning to have all the rooms on one floor swapped with all the rooms two floors below. We were running up and down the stairs all through the night, carrying immaculately pressed uniforms, kit covered in mud, ironing boards and all sorts. Then, at 8am, the corporal told us, 'Not good enough. You're really starting to piss me off. Blah, blah, blah. Change it all back!' And we spent the next five hours changing the rooms back to how they were before.

After spending the evening on my hands and knees, scraping polish off the floor with a bayonet, I phoned my dad. I told him I was having a shit time and finding all the mind games difficult. He didn't know what I was going through, because he was never in the military, so the only advice he could give me was to stick at it. It didn't really matter what he said, though, it was more about me being able to offload, tell someone from outside the situation what a joke it all was. After putting the phone down, and letting everyone else complain to their loved ones, I got straight back to scraping the floor with my bayonet.

Much of what you learn during Commando training is not specific to soldiering. The Royal Marines have something called the Commando Spirit, which is: courage, determination, unselfishness and cheerfulness in the face of adversity. There are signs everywhere, reminding you what the Commando Spirit is, but no one says, 'Today, you are going to learn about courage.' Or, 'Today, you are practising cheerfulness in the face of adversity while you're going down with hypothermia.' (Although you're quite likely to have that experience.) Each recruit naturally absorbs it, through the training. We are training to become the optimum fighting force and go beyond our physical and mental limits. 'It's a state of mind', as the Marine slogan said. The most important training happens in your head rather than your body.

Over the months, you become courageous, determined and unselfish. You learn to always look out for those around you, to have their back before your own. That also ensures that everyone else has your back. You are cheerful in the face of whatever is thrown at you. If you can't see the funny side in scraping polish off the floor with a bayonet, you're not going to last in the Marines. Because it gets a lot worse.

On top of that, there is the professionalism, discipline, integrity, loyalty. Stuff a Marine remembers for the rest of their days, long after they've hung up their boots.

Before passing out, a recruit must complete four final Commando tests, while carrying something like 14 kilograms of equipment and a weapon. The first is an endurance course over Woodbury Common. That's a killer – I battled through miles of tunnels, pools, streams and bogs before running four miles back to camp and completing a shooting test with the standard Marines SA80. Next was a nine-mile speed march.

The third test is the Tarzan assault course – I had 13 minutes to navigate a series of zip wires, high ropes, obstacles and nets, finishing by scaling a nine-metre wall. Finally, there's a 30-mile march over Dartmoor, which I needed to complete in less than eight hours. Once that was all out of the way, our troop boss, and the big boss of the Training Centre, wandered over and handed me my Green Beret and flashes, which are the 'Royal Marines Commando' cloth badges you stitch on to your JWH (jersey wool heavy jumper). I can't say I felt elated. I was cold, wet and, for want of a better word, banjaxed. But I was 'in', which is all that really mattered.

I was just 17 – not legally old enough to drink or vote – and I had just passed one of the toughest infantry training courses in the world, along with only about 10 others of the original 50 recruits. I was now a Royal Marines Commando, a highly trained killing machine, renowned, respected and feared throughout the world.

It was impossible to take in what I'd achieved. The pride in myself only kicked in once I'd got back to the camp and spent time alone with my beret, before the passing out parade. Only then did I begin to take in what that beret stood for. I remember thinking about that Marine five years earlier, in the NAAFI shop. Now I understood why he'd been so dismissive of me. You don't get given the Green Beret. It isn't just a piece of cloth. Being allowed to wear it is a symbol of the kind of man you've become.

From that point on, my whole life would be defined by having earned that right.

CHAPTER 2

By Endurance We Conquer:
Believe In Your Goals

The Royal Marines had three fighting units: 40 Commando in Taunton, 42 Commando in Plymouth and 45 Commando up in Arbroath. I didn't want to go back to Scotland, and 45 Commando spent a lot of time in Norway, freezing their tits off. So I put in for 40 Commando – which trained in jungles and did lots of other exciting stuff I'd seen in the brochures – and got accepted.

A couple of weeks after passing out, I headed over to Taunton one bright Tuesday morning and reported for duty at Norton Manor Camp. And to the corporal on the front gate, I announced,

'Recruit Kane reporting for duty.' He looked me up and down, and said, '*Recruit* Kane? You're a bootneck now, a Marine.'

'Sorry. Marine Kane. Reporting for duty.'

'Just passed out?'

'Yep.'

'Let me just check ...'

The corporal disappeared inside the guardroom and checked some papers, before saying, 'Marine Kane?'

'Yes.'

'It says here you've got a week off and should come back next Tuesday.'

Jesus. I had to lug all my kit to the train station and phone Mum and Dad to tell them I was coming back home. Back in Kilwinning, I spent a few evenings on the beers with my mates, giving it Billy-Big-Bollocks. As I thought I was entitled to do. Then one night I got home and Mum said, 'Your Sergeant Major has phoned from 40 Commando. He says you're AWOL and you've got to get back to Taunton as soon as possible, otherwise they'll send you to jail.'

Whether the corporal at the front gate had made an innocent mistake or played a trick on me – got me 'on a bite', as they say in the Marines – it didn't matter. As far as my Sergeant Major was concerned, it was my fault. I'd spent my entire month's wages on two trains to Scotland and back, plus booze – I was only on £200 as a junior Marine – and I got the mother of all bollockings. And once he'd calmed down, the Sergeant Major said to me, 'Do you know what a donkey bath is?'

'No, sir.'

'You bathe donkeys in them. And there's one over there.'

So it was that I spent my first week as a Marine cleaning up a donkey bath (I assume it was a donkey bath, although I've never seen one since) that was covered in leaves and vines and decades of dirt, while the rest of Alpha Company were doing all the cool soldiering I'd been dreaming about for years.

Luckily, there's only so much donkey bath cleaning you can make a Marine do. And the day after my eighteenth birthday, I flew to Dungannon, Northern Ireland, for my first operational tour. The Troubles had calmed down by the mid-90s, but not completely, so it was still an exciting but unsettling experience. Scotland and Northern Ireland are only separated by about 20 miles of sea so the streets felt very familiar to me, as did the people who lived on them. But to be patrolling those streets with a weapon and live ammunition felt strange. And I'm not sure how useful I'd have been if anything had kicked off. I'd been trained to within an inch of my life, but I still knew little about live soldiering.

The fact that soldiers fight wars was always in the back of my mind, but I didn't really understand why we were in Northern Ireland. I'd grown up with sectarianism, but I never watched the news. As far as I was concerned, I was there to do a job: patrolling, dominating the ground, and disrupting the movement of weapons, ammunition and bomb-making kits. As with everything that's happened in my life since, I just got on with it. The politics was irrelevant. I certainly wasn't in the military for 'Queen and Country', it was all about the challenge and adventure for me.

Having not been a bookish kid, I started reading around this time. One of the first books I read was Ernest Shackleton's *South*, about the great explorer's second expedition to Antarctica and his incredible feat of survival in the most inhospitable of environments. *South* is an extraordinary account of the power of leadership, teamwork and conviction, as well as the story of an individual with incredible personal humility and self-control. It had a significant effect on me.

Shackleton's family motto was *Fortitudine Vincimus* (By Endurance We Conquer). His book made me realise that 'normal' soldiering wasn't going to be enough for me, that I wanted to go further and test myself to the limit. That's why I decided to apply to join the Reconnaissance (Recce) Troop after returning from that first tour in Northern Ireland.

Recce Troops are highly specialised teams, which include a sniper/reconnaissance leader. As the name suggests, a Recce Troop's job is to carry out reconnaissance for its parent

Commando unit, which often means operating behind enemy lines to gather intelligence and prepare the way for the main force. That might mean watching an enemy position for however long is necessary to acquire sufficient information about the area and target/s before going back, picking up 100 men and bringing them back in for the attack. Recce Troop is seen as the elite and, as far as I was concerned, it was the pinnacle of soldiering.

Recce Troops have to become experts in everything: communications, navigation, vehicles and weapons recognition, and all sorts of fieldcraft. There's also the sexy Commando stuff, like climbing, ropework, cliff assaults and skiing. But it was the chance of becoming a sniper that appealed to me most.

I always liked the idea of sneaking about and not being seen and had thought about becoming a sniper since I was 14 or 15, when I made my first ghillie suit in the Cadets. Ghillie suits are what hunters wear when they're stalking deer, and snipers when they don't want to be seen by the enemy – essentially it's meshing covered in pieces of hessian, foliage or whatever else will help them blend in with their surroundings. Essentially, you become a walking bush.

The idea of being able to move through an environment without the enemy seeing you, despite knowing you're there, seemed like the ultimate in soldiering. And to be able to make yourself invisible is all about understanding the environment, and I'd had that connection to nature since I was small.

While I was training at Lympstone, soldiers from different reconnaissance and Special Forces units would descend on the camp to do their elite sniper course. For the most part, the military is about order – starched shirts, trousers perfectly creased, berets sitting at the correct angle – but snipers were the complete opposite. They didn't wear berets and often had long hair. And they'd wander around in their ghillie suits, looking a proper mess. I found them fascinating.

Because Recce Troop is such a specialist thing, I had people saying to me, 'Who the hell do you think you are? You've just joined. You're only 18. And now you're going for Recce selection?' But I just thought, 'Who cares how old I am? I will always show people how good or bad I am at something. I suppose it was a quiet confidence that I would always be able to lead by example.'

That Recce Leaders course, which lasted two weeks, wasn't all sexy Commando stuff though. As part of continuation training, and as we were a troop prone to capture, we then had to do an air crew survival course, which meant going on the run for a fortnight in Cornwall. Without any food. The old adage says that you can go three minutes without air, three days without water and three weeks without food. But people who do go that long without food don't normally get interrogated at the end of it. Thankfully, I managed not to crumble under questioning.

Next was the Royal Navy's Ocean Wave exercise, which had the aim of demonstrating that Britain still had security interests in Asia after Hong Kong was handed back to China in 1997. We were on HMS *Fearless*, whose route took us down the Suez Canal, across the Arabian Sea to Goa and then on to the jungles of Thailand, Brunei and the Philippines, before heading down to South Africa. On that trip, which lasted about eight months, I became a specialist at operating in deserts and jungles and other extreme hostile environments. Suddenly, I was that guy on the cover of the Royal Marines brochure.

I did a lot of boozing on that trip too – we didn't even leave the docks in Egypt – but I was never one for sitting around if there was something more adventurous on the menu. In the Philippines, we had three weeks off, so six or seven of us piled into a Jeepney, which is like a tuk-tuk except bigger, and headed to Baler Bay, which is where the famous surfing scene in *Apocalypse Now* was filmed. That journey took about 16 hours, a lot of it along jungle tracks, but it was more than worth it.

For something like 12 days, we surfed perfect waves and hung out on the beach. We only had our boards and day sacks with us and lived off rations. We didn't even bring hammocks, just slept on the sand. There were a couple of villages nearby, but we barely saw anyone else. Apparently, the locals didn't surf, just like the Robert Duvall character said in the film. So it was just us and the environment: jungle almost down to the beach, a mountain overlooking us and a river running into the sea, which is what created the split in the wave. When the driver turned up to take us back, it was like being dragged away from paradise.

I was only 19 when Ocean Wave ended, but I didn't feel worried. In fact, I knew that as long as I was doing something I really loved and continued to work hard at it, I could achieve pretty much anything. A strong work ethic and a focussed mind are powerful and essential tools for life. There was no magic involved, I just needed to break things down into achievable chunks or steps. I grew on that trip because I saw so many different cultures and lands. I had left the UK and been on my first big adventure, one which shaped the rest of my life and enforced my values.

After Ocean Wave, I joined a two-week Royal Marine sniper selection course, which I passed. The course was at CTCRM Lympstone, where Ross, my twin brother, was now going through training. After finishing school, Ross had spent a couple of years in France with his girlfriend, working as a lifeguard. But when I paid them a visit and told him about my life in the Marines, he packed his bags, came home and signed up.

(Meanwhile, my sister Stroma had joined the RAF.) Ross has always been very focused, so did brilliantly. I thought he was super-brave for making his own tough decision when we were 16, but it was weird seeing him running around and dealing with all the crap I'd had to deal with a few years earlier. Even weirder was him then having to stand to attention to speak to me.

The actual sniper course lasts two-and-a-half months and is renowned throughout the world for its difficulty – the SAS, SBS and Special Forces soldiers from other countries take that course. Any soldier who passes it is considered to be among the elite of the elite. No one shouts at you on the sniper course, because you're already an exceptional soldier. It's more cerebral, about dealing with pressure.

A sniper is a unit on his own. Whereas normal troops are moved around by the companies' individual bosses, pairs of snipers – the shooter and the spotter – are the assets of the Commanding Officer, who's in charge of the entire Commando unit. Snipers are 'force multipliers', which means a pair of them can hold down hundreds of troops, because they can perform more targeted operations.

The first two or three weeks of the course were purely shooting. Every day, we'd be on the range, shooting at targets at a range of one kilometre. It would take at least 10 minutes to walk that distance. As a sniper we would carry the normal service assault rifle, but we would also have a very accurate long-barrelled rifle, often called a sniper rifle. I had been shooting for years since my time in the Cadets at an advanced level of marksmanship. But it wasn't all about the weapons for me. I enjoyed the focus and meditation it required, the peacefulness of mind. American snipers tend to be into their weapons and technology, but I've never met a British sniper like that. They're far more

31

about the reconnaissance and fieldcraft; being at one with the environment; getting into the right position, getting information back and influencing situations. I liked the autonomy, the fact that it was just me and my partner on the battlefield. I liked having to be completely self-sufficient, living or dying by my skills and my wits instead of relying on other people. Pulling the trigger is such a small part of it.

Bear in mind also that as soon as a sniper pulls the trigger and the bullet leaves the end of his rifle, all hell might break loose because he's potentially given his position away. And even if he doesn't pull the trigger, the enemy could still start hammering away at where they think he might be. So a sniper's main role is gathering information and passing it back up the chain, to be used, acted on or dismissed. It's a military truism that time spent in reconnaissance is seldom wasted, which is why snipers are so highly valued.

Doing that course was much more about wanting to improve myself than wanting to kill anyone. Having hated maths at school, I suddenly got very good at trigonometry. I also had to master navigation. When you're going back to pick up 100 men and then bringing them back in, you can't afford to get your navigation wrong. There was also map reading, air photography, weapons and vehicle recognition, memory games and mnemonics, which is basically using acronyms to remember processes.

The most important weapon a sniper has isn't his rifle, it's his power of observation. Snipers have to be hyper-aware of everything around them, because they know that everything is interrelated. It's the 'missing button' concept again, the idea that the most trivial thing might cause disaster. Being a sniper is having the ability to recognise the absence of the normal and the presence of the abnormal. It's also about understanding and helping build 'patterns of life'.

If a sniper is in an observation post watching the enemy, he's building a pattern of life from a snapshot. His reconnaissance will never be, 'There are some people sitting around outside a building.' The bosses need more detail than that. A sniper will remember what those people are wearing, what they're eating, what weapons they're carrying, how many rounds are in their magazines, what their body language is like. A sniper never makes judgements, guesses or assumptions, he has to be specific. For example, if he doesn't know for sure what weapons the enemy is carrying, he might describe them simply as 'long-barrelled rifles'.

The final week of the sniper course consists of badge tests, in all the different disciplines. If you fail one of them, you're off the course – a fail. The stalking test was the toughest. You have about three hours to get into position to take a shot at four directing staff (DS) sitting in deckchairs with binoculars without being spotted. You're dropped off about five kilometers away and have to get within 300 metres of the DS before taking a shot. I'd already done practice stalks and knew I was half-decent at it. Well, I was good enough to crawl right past two people shagging in a car on Woodbury Common without them noticing. Alas, the DS weren't in the throes of passion.

For the test, I was dressed in a pair of combat trousers, with a couple of pads stuffed down the inside and vehicle canvas (the thick material you get on military trucks) glued to the front, because Woodbury Common is covered with sharp gorse and rocks. I had a shooting jacket made specifically for snipers, with pads and a sling hook on the arm, which supports the weapon if you're shooting standing up. Over that was my ghillie suit, my home-made cloak with bits of hessian, old string and other material glued to it, plus my 'head and shoulders'. Every Marine makes a 'head and shoulders' for basic camouflage. It's essentially a bush hat adorned with a piece of scrim net (meshing) with all sorts glued to it. Being able to recognise the shape of a person's head and shoulders is a primeval thing, going right back to when early man feared any lurking stranger. That's why it's essential to conceal that shape by merging it with the background.

The suit had already been roughed up in dirt and buried for a couple of weeks, to weather it. I had cam cream all over my face, and my rifle was also covered in cam cream and tape, so it didn't have any shiny surfaces. My scopes and optics were hooded, and my watch was turned around to stop it reflecting.

Despite all that, a sniper shouldn't need camouflage, at least in theory. They should be skilled enough to close in on the enemy using only the terrain for concealment. There are reasons things get spotted: shape, shine, shadow, silhouette, spacing and sudden movement. Those rules apply to a sniper or an animal not wanting to be seen by a predator, and it's sudden movement that usually gives a sniper's or an animal's position away. That's why any risks on a stalk should be taken early, although you shouldn't really be running anywhere. A sniper has to do everything in a slow, controlled, relaxed way.

You can only do things in a slow, controlled, relaxed way if you've prepared properly and understand the land you're moving across. That means poring over maps and aerial photographs and knowing where the dead ground is. Dead ground might be a valley, which you can't see into and therefore can't judge its distance (judging distance is a separate badge test). You have to know when you can walk, rather than crawl. You have to know where you might breach a hill line or the edge of a ploughed field. You have to know if a field has cows in it, because if you stalk next to it, they might head in your direction. You have to belong to that landscape, be part of it, just like a rock or bush.

Four of us were dropped off at the start of my test, in daylight. And the DS knew we were coming. That was what I loved about it, trying to be invisible to people who knew I was out there. My sniper rifle was in a drag bag slung over my back, along with a set of binoculars, a scope, a notebook, a pen and food rations. I also had an automatic rifle, because if anything did happen for real, I'd need to engage the enemy with that instead of my single-shot sniper rifle. I didn't have anything on my front. Even my pockets had been moved to the back, so that I could access them while crawling. When I stalked, I would keep my sniper rifle in my drag bag until the last minute then swap over my rifles.

Once I started stalking, the other three snipers faded into nothing. It was just me and the land. An 'observer' was walking in and around the area, and in radio contact with the four DS sitting on deckchairs with binoculars. When a DS thinks they've spotted someone, they'll get on the radio to the observer and say, 'Smudge, walk 10 paces to your right. Stop. Put your hand out. Is that a sniper there?' If it is, that sniper is off the course. I've heard stories about people getting their navigation wrong and emerging right in front of the DS. They look up and see four blokes in deckchairs staring back at them. Luckily, I managed to get into a final firing position without being seen.

Getting a shot off is only about 5% of the stalk. But it's an important 5%, not least because there are lots of different things you can fail on. Your position for the shot must be concealed from the enemy and give you cover, which means you need to fire through things rather than over them. If you're covered by a bush, you don't stick your head over or around it, you dig in to see through it – you shoot through cover, never over. The position must be stable enough to support the rifle, which must point naturally at the target. The sight alignment must be spot on, so you're not looking through the scope with shadows on either side. Plus, a bullet doesn't travel in a straight line. It rises out of the barrel, before gravity, drag/friction and wind do their thing. That's where the maths comes in. You must also consider whether your rounds have been in the sun, because the heat will make them fly higher. On a more basic level, you need to know if the barrel is going to lift up when you fire, moving foliage. Or have you used too much oil, so the barrel is going to smoke and give your position away? Not to mention dealing with nerves and adrenaline.

I got a shot away, meaning the DS knew someone was in position. But there was no smoke and no movement, so I remained invisible. The observer signalled that I was in a fair position while taking the shot, which meant I passed the test with 70%. The DS then asked the observer to walk within 10 metres of me. They still couldn't see me, which improved my score by 5%. They asked the observer to walk within five metres of me, before asking me to fire another shot. They still couldn't see me. Up another 5%. The observer walked to within one metre of me, as requested. But they still couldn't see me. Up another 5%. A DS said, 'Put your hand on the sniper's head.' The observer replied, 'Hand going down ... hand on the sniper's head.' Only then did they know where I was. Although that didn't mean they could see me. Then the DS instructed me over the observer's radio, 'Move out of your position.' I managed to move away, still without being seen, which meant I passed with 100%.

It was official: I was one of the best fieldcraft soldiers in the world, just as I'd set out to be, even though I still felt distinctly average.

No one can become that Marine in the jungle overnight. But anyone can apply to become a Marine. Anyone can give the Potential Recruits Course a crack. If you pass that, you know you've got the minerals to have a go at Marines training. Then, if you pass that, you know you've got it in you to pass Recce Troop Selection, which means you've also got it in you to become one of the best trained snipers in the world.

Process and graft – that was what had got me here. It was a simple process in my head – one step at a time in the right direction. From the moment I got on the train to Lympstone without my twin brother, I had been heading into the unknown, pushing myself further and blazing trails. Life was teaching me that I would always be alright, whatever happens . . .

CHAPTER 3

One Bullet, Two Lives Change: Create Your Life Plan

A few years after completing the sniper course, I was in Kuwait, preparing for the invasion of Iraq. I even appeared in a national newspaper back home, decked out in all my sniper gear. The headline read: 'Saddam in his sights'.

When I was waiting to get on that helicopter, to fly into battle for the first time, Saddam Hussein was the last thing on my mind. All sorts of things were going on in my head. I was anxious, scared and super-excited. I think they're all connected. I didn't know what it was going to be like. What it would feel like. What it would look, sound, smell and taste like. But I had to remind myself that I was a professional soldier, that I had been through the most rigorous training in the world. This is what I joined up for. All that training, all that travel, all those experiences I'd had; this was the payback.

The Battle of al-Faw was one of the first battles of the 2003 Iraq War. The coalition objective was to capture key gas and oil platforms plus the Khawr Abd Allah estuary in southern Iraq so that relief vessels could deliver emergency aid and equipment. Having secured the area, the Royal Marines would then capture the rest of the peninsula and move up into Basra.

I was attached to Lima Company, 42 Commando, and our job was to protect 40 Commando against Iraqi forces to the north.

The insertion got off to a bad start when, due to the weather, a US Sea Knight helicopter crashed in Kuwait while Lima Company were assembling on the ground, killing four Americans and eight of our men, including members of the Brigade Recce unit. The Americans then called off the insertion because the visibility was so bad, meaning we were stuck in the desert for hours while we worked out what had happened to the downed helicopter (or 'helo' as we called them).

Eventually, we were picked up by British helos, each rammed to the gunwales with munitions. I was tooled up as well – nearly all of my operational weight was ammunition, grenades, mines and optics. I vividly remember looking through a little porthole window as we flew over the site of the stricken Sea Knight, smashed to smithereens, a smouldering wreck. I glanced at my old mate Daz Phillips, who I'd known for years and was also staring down at the crash site. Sitting directly opposite me, I could barely see him over the quad bike rammed with ammunition resupplies and his massive operational Bergan (rucksack). The look on his face mirrored mine. 'So,' that look said, 'this is what war is really about.'

As we landed, the rotors kicked up a sandstorm around us. The rear hatch was already lowered and we jumped out into the LS (landing site) and this thick, black, gloopy quick sand. Daz and I were in it almost up to our knees because of the weight of our operational Bergans, and it was hard to get into cover behind the sand bank. As the helo took off again, the mortar rounds started winging in and I looked back to see Daz still knee-deep in the mud, right out in the open. I ditched my kit, legged it back and helped him with his gargantuan pack. And once we'd made it back into cover, we started laughing like crazy. At the time, I didn't know what we were laughing at. Only later did I realise it was a nervous response.

The first time coming under attack in Iraq was not what I expected. I've often felt like that. During my first night up on Woodbury Common during Commando training, I remember lying there thinking, 'This is exciting and bloody brilliant, it's what I wanted to be doing. But it isn't what I thought it would be like.' It was the same the first time I went up in a plane, and the first time I shot a deer on a stalk.

I thought the attack would be louder. The sound of a bullet being fired is a crack followed by a thump. The crack is the bullet passing by your ear at supersonic speed, the thump is the hammer hitting the pin, creating the explosion that sends the bullet on its way. But I expected more than cracks and thumps. The mortars and artillery really got to me, because they are so loud and indiscriminate. You hear them whistling over the top of you and think 'phew' as they land and explode elsewhere. It's when they whistle then suddenly stop that is terrifying, because it usually means they are coming straight down on top of you.

When they're in the middle of a firefight, Royal Marines are so well drilled that they don't have to think. 'Train hard, fight easy' is the maxim. When the shit hits the fan, and things are happening in a way we hadn't planned for, we can see a way through without having to process things. That gives us the headspace to be able to work out how to attack the situation. Most people don't react like that. If you aren't trained to be a soldier and everything kicks off, you're likely to freeze or go straight into flight mode: denial, deliberation, decision. In times of crisis, most people experience a denial phase ('This can't be happening!'), followed by deliberation ('What the hell should I do?'), *then* a decision process (and the decision probably won't be the right one). But a Marine can ignore those first two phases and go straight to making decisions in the form of rapid, direct action. That's what training does. You are so well drilled that you're able to change/flex when things don't go to plan, which they rarely do. That's why another popular tenet is: 'No plan survives first contact with the enemy'.

No amount of training can stop you getting shot. But you've got a much better chance of not getting shot if you do everything right. And I always thought getting shot was fair game, because it involved a level of skill from the other side. However, while we were being mortared and the rounds were whistling in and coming down around us, I remember thinking how unfair it all seemed. I hated the idea that you could do everything right and still get killed. It felt indiscriminate, almost as if the other side was cheating (even though we were doing the same thing).

Once we'd extracted ourselves, my partner and I swept up through the battlefield, making our way stealthily across an area that had been fought over for years. There were UXO – unexploded ordinance/munitions – everywhere from the coalition's 'shock and awe bombardment', and that's when the navigation skills came into their own. We pushed out two or three kilometres in front of Lima Company, providing an early warning sniper screen for the unit. And we were on our own. After establishing an observation post in an old bombed-out rubble pile, offering good cover from view and from fire, we surrounded our position with mines. Without anyone to get us out of the shit if things went wrong, those mines were effectively our back-up. If anyone came close, we'd activate a firing device (otherwise known as a 'clacker') and that would probably be the end of them.

In our observation post, my partner and I took one hour on and one hour off. We were part of a sniper screen, three sniper pairs across the front of the unit, and it was our job to let the rest of the unit know what was coming up and down the road we overlooked. That night, I watched the Iraqis launch a rocket. It wobbled upwards, cleared the forest line and headed in the direction of Kuwait. More specifically, Camp Coyote, where we were just based.

In truth, it was a one-sided affair. The Americans had smashed the hell out of the place and there were Iraqi ambulances everywhere.

It was several days later when the time finally came to do the thing that all snipers have to do, what you might call the sharp end of a mission. The pulling of the trigger, that small action that would change my life and the target's.

We were on the edge of a date palm plantation and had just come under contact from the enemy. They had jimmy-rigged RPGs to explode mid-air instead of on impact, winging above us and between our vehicles, exploding randomly. We pulled back to a safer position to allow us to clear the wood line properly. The rest of the Company swung round, lined out and 'advanced to contact' – deliberately advancing in the direction of the enemy until you draw fire. My partner and I held a position on the flank. Our main job was observation. I could see friendly faces through my scope as I scanned the distant treeline for enemy positions. I noticed a great mate, Stuart 'Shiner' Wright, sweating hard as they advanced.

As a sniper I am searching for shape, shine, shadow, silhouette, spacing and sudden movement. It was sudden movement that caught my eye. I saw men busying themselves on a rooftop half a kilometre away, in the direction Shiner and the men were advancing. Years of training had allowed for the cool and calculated evaluation of the situation as we completed the final checks.

'Take the shot,' said my boss over the radio. And I did.

It was my first shot as a sniper in battle and I knew it was on target, the vortex spun away from me and the target dropped.

Out of the corner of my eye, I saw Shiner hit the deck. He'd heard the crack and thought someone might be shooting at him. It's hard to say what would have happened had I not taken that shot.

Being a sniper seems cold and merciless, which is why people assume we're sociopaths. Psychopaths, even. Throughout the history of modern warfare, snipers have been seen as underhand. Not above board like an honest pitched battle, out in the open. I can understand that. A single sniper can wreak havoc on a force of 100 men. Never mind the casualties, just the threat and fear of an unseen enemy can be hugely demoralising. That's why when snipers get caught, they're not usually treated well.

But for me, it was never about any of that. Yes, I liked being in control. But it was the stalking that I loved most, the fieldcraft that enabled me to get close enough to kill the enemy and withdraw without being detected. To be able to do that, you have to be a master of camouflage and concealment, be able to survive and thrive in hostile environments, prove your expertise, demonstrate that you understand everything around you. Yes, I was also trained to shoot people from a long distance away. But that was just part of it.

A sniper's job is never done once he's pulled the trigger, because he then has to get the hell out of Dodge, which meant picking our way through mines and unexploded bombs, not only from the Iran–Iraq War two decades earlier, but also from the recent shock American bombardment. On top of that, we were worried about being strafed by the Americans, who wouldn't necessarily know who we were. But whether the Americans saw us or not, we managed to make it back unscathed.

That shot prompted me to think about life more deeply. Which isn't always a good thing as a soldier. We'd gone into Iraq, caused chaos and I'd managed to stay alive. And when nothing happens to you, in terms of physical damage, it's easy to write it off as a non-event. It's easy to think, 'It was only life-changing for other people because they got shot or blown-up. But I got through it alright, so it makes no sense to dwell on it.' But after a few more months in Iraq, I realised that I didn't want to do this anymore. Life's too short. I might feel okay now, but I worried that if I stayed in for another 10 years, I'd risk mental damage. Some soldiers sign up to the military to go to war, but not me. I knew there were other things I should be doing.

Scud missiles landing all around you, while you're wondering if they might follow up with chemical weapons, isn't pleasant. But the amount of contact I experienced in Iraq was nothing compared to what my mates went through later. By the end of 2003, we'd deposed Saddam Hussein and it felt like job done. Little did I know that the war would still be raging almost a decade on. Meanwhile, my old unit 40 Commando went out to Afghanistan and got smashed for six months, with lots of fatalities. People didn't just die over there, they also came home with all sorts of mental trauma.

I hadn't seen much action compared to others, but it was enough for me to grasp how easily life can be snuffed out.

Back on Scottish soil, I spent a lot of time thinking about the things I'd seen. Like an Iraqi guy I came across lying on the ground, surrounded by his sobbing wife and kids. I couldn't work out why he was dying until I lifted him up as part of a primary/

secondary survey and everything fell out of his back, through the gaping exit wound. Or the four dead guys we found on the side of a road, with their half-eaten last meal. As I buried them in the sand, I asked myself: 'Why didn't the sands of time run out for me?' It hit home to me that even at best, life is short and incredibly fragile.

I wouldn't describe it as post-traumatic stress disorder (PTSD) – I wasn't having nightmares or flashbacks – it was more a case of trying to make some kind of sense of the things I'd seen and done. I'd always been quite pragmatic about death. When Mum switched jobs from midwife to paramedic and ended up in the same ambulance as my dad, they'd talk very matter-of-factly about the jobs they'd been on over dinner, which might have involved picking up body parts after someone had been hit by a train. I'd seen nothing compared to what my parents had experienced over the years. But I also knew those six months in Iraq weren't normal and had affected me. So I booked up to see a psychologist, something I knew was necessary.

I needed to get ahead of things, get stuff off my chest before it was too late. Because if I didn't talk, I was worried stuff would come back and haunt me somewhere down the line; you're just kicking the can down the street, as they say. Soldiers pride themselves on being big, strong superhumans so they don't talk about the experiences that haunt them. That's what ends up breaking them. I've seen that happen so many times to old mates who seemed invincible. They had the drive to become Marines in the first place and learned so many skills. But they lose something and are never able to find it again. I needed to sort through the things in my head, to 'normalise' what I had experienced and clarify what needed to happen next.

★　　★　　★

Having smashed his Marines training and won the King's Badge for best recruit, my twin brother Ross was now an adventure training instructor, teaching mountaineering, kayaking and all the other outdoor stuff we both loved in the Marines. (Ross was climbing Everest with a Marines expedition team when he heard about the helicopter going down in Kuwait, killing Recce and snipers. It was several days before he found out I was alive, and the not knowing messed him up quite a bit.) And now I wanted to be doing the same as Ross. That adventure stuff was the main reason I joined the Marines, and I'd been thinking about making a career of it for a couple of years already.

A year earlier, in the summer of 2002, I'd led an expedition of schoolchildren into the interior of Guyana for an adventure travel company called World Challenge. I was only 24 but had been a Marine for eight years, so I guess I knew enough about surviving and thriving in hostile environments. I was in the middle of the jungle with these 16 kids from Slough for four weeks and I loved watching them go from normal, disorganised teenagers – leaving kit lying around, losing stuff, missing the transport – to mini survival experts, who were able to prep their food, keep their kit dry, put a hammock up and do bits of first aid.

Towards the end of the expedition, we yomped to Kaieteur Falls, which is the world's biggest single-drop waterfall in terms of volume of water. It was a beautiful sight – the dirty Potaro River drops off a cliff more than 200 metres high and 100 metres wide, into the jungle below. There might even have been a rainbow. But when I looked at the kids, they didn't seem interested. Looking back, it was understandable. They'd been in the jungle for weeks, slowly rotting away. They were knackered and bored and probably just wanted to relax and watch some TV. But at the time, it didn't sit right with me.

It would be too dramatic to say my life flashed before me, but I suspected that in no time at all, this moment would be a distant memory. My future held humdrum responsibilities, as a husband, a father and an employee. Water is a good example of life passing by; it stops for nothing. So I got the kids to sit on the edge of the waterfall and close their eyes. I told them to listen to the noise of it, feel the spray on their faces, flare their nostrils and take in the jungle smells. Then I said to them, 'Imagine you're back in Slough and it's the next school term. You've just come in from lunch, you've got double maths. You're bored and staring out of the window at the pouring rain. Now, open your eyes! Trust me, you're going to want to be here, instead of in that classroom.' The kids thought that was amazing. I did, too. Mindfulness wasn't really a thing in 2002, but I was doing it without knowing it. It was about making the most of the moment. Not just *being* there but savouring it. Caressing it, smelling it, hearing it, eating and drinking it up.

Shortly after returning from Iraq, I led another expedition of kids to Bolivia. That was the trip that cemented my future. I loved putting my survival skills into practice and imparting that knowledge. I thought I could quite easily do that sort of stuff full-time, so I booked myself on to as many adventure training courses as I could cram into my time off, whether it was climbing, mountaineering, kayaking or whatever. But I kept being told I couldn't put in for longer courses during my leave. That pissed me off and I even ended up booking myself on courses without my boss' permission. I didn't like being controlled in what was supposed to be my own time. I'd joined the Marines as a boy but was now a man. I was more curious, more aware of what the world had to offer. And I was questioning things. That doesn't really work in the military.

It was like the final stages of a relationship. I'd been madly in love with the idea of being a Royal Marines Commando since I was 12 years old and had spent 10 years being one. The Marines gave me the skills to thrive at whatever I decided to do next, and now I felt the need to leave and do something else. I didn't feel any acrimony towards the Marines, and they felt none towards me. We'd grown apart, so I put in my notice to leave.

The best thing I ever did was join the Marines. And, in hindsight, the second-best thing I ever did was to leave the Marines. But it didn't feel like that at the time – it really scared me. I was 26 and still at the top of my game, at least theoretically. Marines have the confidence and swagger to go with the Green Beret and the Commando Flashes. When you're a Marine, you never walk anywhere on your own, you always feel like you've got 6,000 lads behind you. Conversely, when you leave, you feel very much alone.

I could easily have worked for another 15 years, taken the monthly pay cheques and then the pension. And I could hardly believe I was leaving. Something was compelling me to go forwards into uncertainty and I was excited by the prospect, but I had no back-up now. I'd left that incredible brotherhood and would have to work things out for myself.

Ready to face failure or success, I had jumped out of my comfort zone looking for new places to explore and new challenges to meet. The clock was ticking.

CHAPTER 4

Digging In My Own Backyard: 'We Become What We Think About'

I earned something like £1,500 for each of the expeditions to Guyana and Bolivia (which was more than the Marines were paying me), so I thought I could make an honest living out of it. But having left the military armed to the teeth with outdoor activity qualifications, I soon realised there wasn't much work about for someone with those skills. What work there was involved doing 16-hour days for next to nothing, and I'd had quite enough of that already.

I needed to earn money and I wasn't shy of graft so a couple of months after leaving the Marines, I found myself being interviewed for a job as a gas and electricity salesman. There wasn't much of the old Marines swagger when I walked into *that* building – not least because a seagull had just shat on my face.

Even thinking about that interview is excruciating. I'd obviously scrubbed the seagull shit off my cheek, but there was a big stain on my polyester demob suit and I stank of fish. Then the interviewers made me do a chicken dance. There were four of them behind the desk, watching me bop around to 'The Birdie Song', apparently to see if I had 'the confidence for sales'. I was one of the most skilled soldiers in the world. I'd led expeditions into some of the most challenging terrains in the world.

Humiliating doesn't even begin to cover it. But worse was to come: the bastards gave me the job.

I was one of those annoying people who goes door to door trying to persuade people to switch their energy supplier. I felt incredibly uncomfortable and embarrassed doing that job. I was working with some very unpleasant characters. They even taught me techniques to get through a potential customer's door: look down, wipe your feet and point at their crotch. Apparently, that's the door-to-door salesman's version of 'open sesame'. But it rarely worked for me. I might have been half-decent at dancing to 'The Birdie Song', but I was terrible at selling energy. Strangely, the two don't necessarily go hand in hand.

The final straw was when a man slammed his door in my face and told me to piss off. I pulled off my company fleece without unzipping it, ripped off my logoed shirt and threw them on the path, before frisbeeing my clipboard into next door's garden. But I couldn't even do that properly. When I got back to my car, I realised I'd left the keys in the fleece and had to go back and get them.

Around this time, loads of ex-soldiers, many of them Marines and Special Forces, were heading back to the Middle East to earn megabucks as private security. I was up on the roof of the new house I'd just bought in Glasgow, doing some repairs, when my mate Ross Johnson, who was also a sniper in the Marines, phoned and asked if I fancied joining him in Iraq. It was a very tempting offer, something like £2,000 a week. And it wasn't just the money, the excitement was also tempting. But doing private security in warzones is arguably more dangerous than soldiering, and I couldn't help thinking, 'Maybe they're not really getting paid megabucks, maybe they're just getting paid early.' So I knocked Ross' offer back, along with quite a few others. A couple of years later, my mate 'Shiner' (the guy who hit the deck when I took that shot in Iraq) was killed in Iraq, as were a few others.

Burying Shiner was a tough gig and it brought reality crashing down on me. I didn't want to die in an IED or getting shot; if I was going to go, I wanted it to be by misadventure in some far-flung land, while doing something epic.

While security work didn't appeal, I'd also been hearing about ex-Marines earning 40 or 50 grand for half a year's work on oil rigs. These guys sounded quite romantic – maverick rope and climbing experts grafting for six months but with plenty of spare time to enjoy their money and with nobody shooting at them. So with some of my resettlement cash from the Marines, I did a rope access course, before getting my rope and inspection engineer qualifications. Unfortunately, all the jobs were sewn up, so that was another dead end.

I eventually managed to land a job with an organisation in Glasgow called Skill Force, which involved military instructors going into schools and teaching disaffected kids. I was working with military dudes – ex-sergeant majors and people marking time before leaving – and it felt like we were making a difference to those kids' lives. They weren't bad kids, many of them just hadn't had a good start. So a lot of what we did was behaviour management, using our softer military skills to get through to them when their teachers couldn't.

I didn't have many GCSEs, but I was highly educated in other ways. I'd been around the world umpteen times, lived in jungles and deserts. My knowledge about the world and its people was second to none, but I was just starting to learn about myself. I was hit by this tremendous hunger for learning. It was almost a period of mania. You might argue I've never come out of it.

It all started when I came across a *Guardian* supplement about entrepreneurs in the Skill Force staffroom. That led me to Napoleon Hill's *Think and Grow Rich*, which consists of interviews with some of the most successful people in America in the early twentieth century and was one of the first self-help books. Hill's most famous quote is, 'We become what we think about'. That really resonated with me – I'd seen it throughout my Marine training, the power of mental strength and determination to achieve. Losing starts in the mind and I was able to pinpoint all of my 'successes' to specific times when I'd made a decision based on my thinking. The things that consumed my mind had become my reality; I had made them happen.

I also read *The Strangest Secret* by Earl Nightingale, which preaches that anyone can have what they want, and a mind is like a garden: take care of it and it will flourish, neglect it and it will become overgrown with weeds. And there was 'Acres of Diamonds', an essay by Russell H. Conwell. It's the story of a farmer who buys a plot of land, digs a bit and finds nothing, before setting off on a fruitless search for gems. Meanwhile, the person he sold that first plot of land to stuck around for years and found a rich seam of diamonds. The moral being that people think opportunity, contentment and happiness come from elsewhere, and spend all their time chasing it. But it's often right under your feet and can only be unearthed as a result of time and hard work. To borrow a phrase from Conwell, it's about 'digging in your own backyard'.

Maybe the most important book I read was *Meditations* by Roman emperor and Stoic philosopher Marcus Aurelius. It's pretty deep stuff but written in an accessible way, so that I could recognise myself in its pages. The Marines had already taught me a lot of the lessons, without me knowing it (it's no coincidence that Marcus Aurelius was also a military man). A central theme of the book is the idea that good and bad things don't happen, it's only your judgement that makes them 'good' or 'bad'. That's such a powerful message, because it means people can only do you harm if you allow that to happen.

Then there's the quote: 'How short it is from birth until dissolution'. In other words, don't waste what little time you have. All this information – a wise man's life's work – cost about seven quid.

I read a lot of books about how to achieve success in business, including volumes by Henry Ford and the industrialist Andrew Carnegie. But it was never about the money for me – I didn't dream of flash cars and big houses. It was about being single-minded and getting what I wanted from life, understanding that whatever anyone spends their time thinking about becomes their reality.

Money is nice. It's helpful, and you need enough to cover the basics, but it's not as valuable as time. Money comes and goes, time only goes. Once that's gone, you can never get it back. It's a heavy thought – I had a lot of heavy thoughts while I was on that voyage of discovery – such as 'we're all dying'. Some people will die today, everyone else will die at some random point in the future. No one knows how long they've got left. So why would you wait to do whatever it is you want to do? Waiting is precious time wasted.

I'd been going out and pushing myself to get what I wanted since I was a kid. I didn't wait until I was 18 before joining the Marines. I didn't wait to do the Recce Troop Selection course or the sniper course, and I didn't wait to get out of the Marines. Floodgates opened and life suddenly seemed too brief to be messing around. I had to grab hold of it with both hands and wring it dry.

It was an exciting time, but it was also confusing. I had a house and a stable job that paid decent money, but I couldn't help thinking I'd drifted into that situation, that there was much more in life I could be doing. At this time, it became apparent that there were zero prospects of progression with Skill Force. It was a comfortable living, and I enjoyed it, but I certainly didn't want to be doing it for another 30 or 40 years. So one night, I sat down and tried to figure out what diamonds I had in my own backyard. I concluded I had two main assets: my rope and inspection certificates and the time those certificates could create for me if I managed to find work on an oil rig, where I'd work two weeks on and two weeks off.

I took a day off work, headed up to Aberdeen and went around all the offshore companies again with my CV. I landed an interview, managed to avoid getting shat on by a seagull and got the job. But having quit Skill Force and relocated, it wasn't exactly what I expected. For a start, it was onshore. And there wasn't any ropework. It was mainly touring fabrication shops and inspecting welds on metal and pipework before it went out to the oil rigs. At night, I spent a lot of time in my B&B, thinking, 'What the hell have I done?'

It seemed that all the companies wanted you to have offshore experience before giving you an offshore job. But how could I gain experience if no one would give me a job? I knew I had the necessary skills, and I'd picked up all the lingo in Aberdeen, I'd just never applied them to an oil rig, so the only way forward seemed to be to 'rework' my CV. It worked. I managed to land a job with RBG, an offshore rope access and maintenance company.

The 14-day contract was for £300 a day, working on Shell's giant Brent Delta oil and gas platform over 160 kilometers north-east of the Shetland Islands. On my first day, I arrived at the heliport, climbed into an immersion suit, jumped on the helicopter and tried my best to look like it was all old hat to me. When we landed on the rig, I felt quite overwhelmed. Not because I'd never been on an oil rig before, but because I was doing something I'd spent so much time thinking about.

I enjoyed it on that oil rig at first. Like the jungle or the desert, it was a whole new environment to test myself in. Every morning, I'd do derrick inspections – a derrick being the framework supporting the drilling apparatus. I'd climb up – there was no lift – rig the ropes and then abseil down over a period of a few hours, checking nuts and bolts and for any loose objects; they called it a dropped object survey. It didn't really feel like work, not least because health and safety regulations meant I hardly did any. After the check, I'd head back to the bear pit, where all the scaffolders and rope access guys hung out, and put my feet up for an hour or so. After a cup of tea and some biscuits, I'd maybe head back out to put barriers around the worksite, before getting my paperwork done and heading back to the bear pit for lunch.

Right at the start of that job, I wrote in my diary that I'd work on the rigs for no more than three years. I'd calculated that that was long enough to earn the necessary money, do enough thinking and claw back enough time, working two weeks on and two weeks off. During my time onshore, I planned to go climbing or skiing in the Alps, retrain and get the necessary outdoor qualifications and brush up on my skills. Offshore, I'd read on the helicopter, I'd read on the running machine, I'd read in my little cabin, while some scaffolder was snoring in the bed above. Sometimes I'd read all through the night, while scribbling down plans and business ideas, some more inspired than others.

For example, back in Glasgow, I'd noticed how the streets were covered in chewing gum, so I bought a chewing gum removal machine for about £4,000. Outside the local cinema, I circled each piece of chewing gum with chalk and took pictures, before sending the pictures to the manager and telling him I could get rid of it all for 500 quid. To my surprise, they asked me to come down and do it. I didn't make any money from my short-lived chewing gum removal business, but it was a learning process, like most apparent failures are. It made me understand more clearly that I needed to do something that was close to my heart and pour everything into it.

After a year or so offshore, I was growing weary of life on the rig. I desperately missed the camaraderie of the Marines, the fun and the banter, doing exceptional things as part of an exclusive club. Instead of everyone looking out for each other, the offshore world was full of bitching and back-stabbing. And everyone just seemed so lazy. I'd get taken aside and told not to work so fast, because I was making them look bad. Jobs that could have been finished in a few days were dragged out for weeks. I wasn't used to that way of working. In the military, you do any job to the best of your ability and as quickly as you can.

As a result, I was chafing to leave, scared of getting caught up in the cushy lifestyle and becoming lazy – the offshore trap. I could easily envisage a couple of years suddenly turning into 10. And if you've been working offshore for 10 years, that means five years of living on rigs, festering in the bear pit, sitting in your own special seat, watching *Deadliest Catch* on the Discovery Channel every night, wishing away time before sloping off to bed. I might end up in an old people's home one day, but I didn't really fancy being in one in my thirties.

Future Commandos in the making. Me and Ross on one of our first mountain days climbing the Cobbler in Arrochar with Dad. Later in life, we would both be based at Faslane naval base just down the road from this picture. 1982.
(Twelve years on I would join the Marines.)

Marine Kane PO52850R. I joined the Royal Marines at the age of 16 and passed out as a Commando at 17 years old. Shortly after this I was deployed to Northern Ireland with 40 Commando. 1995.

Abseiling out of a helicopter onto the back deck of HMS *Fearless* in 1997, somewhere in the South China Sea deployed with 40 Commando Recce Troop.

In the Malay jungle in 1997 on a three-week survival course. Here I am making a rattan fish trap. The skills I learned here at 19 years old have served me well in my life.

Train hard, fight easy. Grizzing it out on a three-week international patrolling competition in Curacao, 1998. Rarely in life does anything of value come without toil.

24 years old and leading expeditions in South American jungles. Understanding mindfulness for the first time in Guyana, Kaieteur Falls, 2002.

42 Commando, L Coy sniper deployed in Iraq, 2003. Observation skills are one of the biggest assets of the sniper who are the eyes and ears of the unit.

Mid-contact in Iraq, 2003 with one of the burning oil wells in the background. Being in a contact is a surreal experience.

Climbing Long Curved Ridge on Buachaille Etive Mòr. One of the most iconic mountains in Scotland and my old stomping ground. 2005.

The man, the myth, the legend – my twin brother Ross and fellow Royal Marines Commando in Bavaria where he was based. 2007.

Repairing a wind turbine blade in Wales. Rope access is usually a glamorous way of accessing a shit job. Being outside working has always been in my DNA. 2009.

Working offshore gave me the lifestyle I wanted to be able to build my qualifications and experience in the outdoors. Two weeks working then two weeks off. Skydiving, 2010. Photo Rob Franklin GBCT.

Testing stunts in Norway for *71 Degrees North* in 2011. I rigged this Tyrolean traverse above a 100-metre drop to the fjord below.

Me and Henry Cavill driving across one of the most hostile environments on earth, the Taklamakan Desert in Northwest China, dubbed the desert of death. *Driven to Extremes*, 2012.

Exiting an Ebola treatment centre in Sierra Leone, 2014. The decontamination process had over 30 steps including this initial chlorine rinse. One mistake could literally cost you your life.

Me and my younger brother Struan on Tier 2 above the boulder field in Mount Nyiragongo volcano filming *One Strange Rock* in 2016. You can just see the vent that was erupting behind us which ultimately killed my plans of getting to the bottom on this expedition.

Thankfully, becoming a supervisor on the ropes led to other things onshore. Through a mate, the St Enoch Centre shopping mall in Glasgow asked if I could change their lightbulbs and clean all the sockets. I'd used the money from working on the rigs to buy a couple of ropes and harnesses, and that was effectively my first job as my own company. Soon, I was doing any job that required rope access. Cleaning windows, changing lead flashing on roofs, bridge inspections, clearing pigeon shit from buildings, putting pigeon spikes on buildings. In no time, I had four or five people working for me. I wasn't getting rich from it, but I'd located the diamonds – which had been right under my feet the whole time – and started digging in earnest.

We started putting up met masts for the wind industry (met masts contain instruments that record the weather, to help energy companies decide if they're going to erect wind turbines or not). My little brother Struan was part of the gang, and Ross, who had now also left the Marines, was sometimes on board as well. We then got involved with constructing and cleaning the actual turbines, all over Scotland.

It was time to stop working offshore. The day I flew off my last rig was exactly three years after I started my first rig job, just as I'd predicted. I knew I wouldn't miss it, and that being a businessman wasn't really me either. I missed getting out in the wild. Then a door opened on to a whole new world I didn't even know existed.

One day in 2010, a guy phoned me out of the blue, asking probably the strangest question I've ever been asked: 'Could you get a film crew into an active volcano?'

CHAPTER 5

Inside the Volcano: Outside Your Comfort Zone

Alex ran an outfit that offered health and safety advice to TV production companies. He'd heard about me from a friend of a friend, knew I was an ex-Marine and was handy with ropes.

A couple of weeks later, I went down to London and met Alex for coffee at Caffè Nero, Goodge Street – life-changing moments happen in the most mundane places. Over a couple of cappuccinos, he explained the gig: a BBC film crew was making a documentary called *Richard Hammond's Journey to the Centre of the Planet*. The plan was to film scientists collecting lava samples from inside an active volcano called Mount Nyiragongo, in the Democratic Republic of the Congo. My job would be to make sure they got in and out safely. I couldn't believe I'd been asked to do such a cool job, so immediately said yes. Because that's what I do.

The Congo gig obviously sounded adventurous – and quite dangerous – but exactly how adventurous and dangerous didn't really register. All I could think about right then was kit, logistics and costs. But something of great significance took place that day. Since leaving the Marines, I'd been on my hands and knees for years, spinning that drill and trying to raise a new fire inside. Now, some guy I didn't know had wandered up behind me and blown tinder into those embers.

I had a few months to plan while I was still working long hours on the turbines. The last job before I flew to the Congo was cleaning oil spills from inside two turbines at a McVitie's biscuit factory. Take away the abseiling and there's nothing appealing about cleaning oil from inside a wind turbine. It was summer, hot as an oven and I almost collapsed with heat stroke. There was no clever gadgetry involved, it was just Struan and I with cloths and bottles of cleaning fluid.

By now, I had several teams working for me and was earning good enough money to do lots of fun things in my spare time. But when you could be abseiling into a volcano, cleaning inside a wind turbine doesn't really cut it.

I'd long been fascinated by the Congo and this part of central Africa. I'd seen documentaries about the jungle and the endangered mountain gorillas that lived there and read up on the history, including Henry Morton Stanley's two books about his nineteenth-century exploration of the Congo and involvement in the Belgian colonisation. Stanley was a terrible man, a racist and murderer, and Belgium's leaders, including the atrocious King Leopold II, were worse.

After Leopold acquired rights to the 'Congo Free State' in 1885, the Congolese were forced to work on rubber plantations, beaten, mutilated and killed indiscriminately. Millions died of disease and overwork. The Congo gained independence from Belgium in 1960, but it didn't improve things for most of its people. Under the spectacularly corrupt dictator Mobutu Sese Seko, the Congo (or Zaire as he renamed it) fell into ruin.

In neighbouring Rwanda, a genocide happened 34 years after independence but was largely down to Belgium's colonial legacy. The Tutsis and Hutus had ancient bonds and shared the same language and culture. There had always been differences between them in terms of social status, but it was the Belgians who strictly divided them into ethnic groups, favouring the Tutsis. When Tutsi rebels seized power in neighbouring Rwanda in 1994, more than a million Hutus escaped to Zaire, fearing revenge for the estimated 800,000 Tutsis killed in the 100-day genocide. Tens of thousands of them died of cholera around the city of Goma, which is about 19.3 kilometres from Mount Nyiragongo, and mass graves were filled.

In 1996, Rwandan forces invaded Zaire, triggering the first Congo War. Mobutu was deposed the following year, and Zaire became the Democratic Republic of the Congo again. But civil wars have raged throughout the country since – apparently the most deadly conflict since World War Two. The area around Mount Nyiragongo crawls with Mai-Mai militia and Congolese and Rwandan rebels, as well as criminal gangs dealing in black market charcoal and fish. The Congo has never managed to shrug off its image as Africa's 'heart of darkness', as the writer Joseph Conrad christened it.

I knew that the trip would be challenging but I tried to rationalise things and kept telling myself that I'd spent 10 years as a Marine, been to war, travelled the world and led expeditions. I also assumed the BBC wouldn't be sending a film crew anywhere too dangerous, so I got planning. But I couldn't shake the anxiety.

We flew into Kigali, the capital city of Rwanda, where we paid the necessary 'motivation' to get over the border into the Congo, before travelling to our hotel in Goma, the closest city to Mount Nyiragongo. Our group consisted of Alex from the safety company, who was also the paramedic, then me and an old mate from the Marines called Mike Francis. (A four-person BBC film crew and the scientists they were filming would follow on in a few days.)

We also had a fixer, and one of the first things he said to us was, 'Be careful if you leave your hotel.' But Mike and I were restless after our long journey and wanted to stretch our legs, take in a bit of the local vibe and get a few extra supplies . . .

The Democratic Republic of the Congo is one of the poorest countries in the world and in Goma, at that time, it was impossible to know who was good and who was bad. There were weapons and bad vibes everywhere and it's not the place to be going for an afternoon stroll. The atmosphere in Goma was one of the most intense I had ever felt.

No sooner had we left the hotel than we were stopped by three guys on mopeds, claiming to be secret police. Within seconds, we were surrounded by a huge crowd, some of them carrying AK-47s. When these 'secret police' put us against a wall and took our wallets, before telling us they had to take us in for questioning, Mike and I feared the worst.

These guys were dressed in vests and Bermuda shorts and had no ID. They could have been anyone, and things could escalate extremely quickly in Goma – flash to bang in seconds, as the Marines say – so we didn't really want to stick around to find out. We were a couple of hundred metres from the water of Lake Kivu, so tried to edge in that direction as we quietly discussed legging it and jumping in. But with the crowd around us growing, we decided to tell the guys our ID was back at the hotel and we started walking in that direction, knowing the crowd would act as a shield of sorts.

When we arrived back at the hotel, our fixer appeared looking annoyed, before fetching our ID and letting the 'secret police' photograph it. We then had to pay a lot of money in 'fines'. But at least it got rid of them. It was an important lesson: it didn't matter what I'd achieved in the Marines, if I didn't do what I was told and take the necessary precautions in the Congo, things could get catastrophic quickly. My career in TV could quite easily have lasted a single afternoon.

The following morning, we drove the 19.3 kilometers to the base of Mount Nyiragongo, in Virunga National Park. Nyiragongo is 3,470 metres high and part of a string of volcanoes just north of Goma and Lake Kivu. Its main rim is about a couple of kilometres in circumference and the lava lake inside is 500 metres deep, making it the largest and most active lava lake in the world. Surrounded by jungle on all sides, where about half of the known population of the mountain gorillas still live, Nyiragongo is just like what a volcano looks like in cartoons, with a glowing halo and an almost constant plume of noxious gases escaping from the top. But there's nothing comical about it. Nyiragongo and the neighbouring Nyamuragira are responsible for almost half of Africa's volcanic eruptions. While Nyiragongo is a 'shield volcano' rather than a 'Strombolian volcano' – meaning that it doesn't blast lava into the air – its lava is so pure and thin (which is why scientists want to study it) that the hot molten rock flows fast, like water, covering huge areas very quickly. In 2002, Nyiragongo erupted twice, sending a stream of lava up to a kilometre wide right through the middle of Goma, destroying almost half the city. Over 200 people died through the effects of the eruption and the accompanying carbon dioxide release.

At the base of Mount Nyiragongo is an old, rickety observatory and station manned by a few park rangers. There wasn't much in this observatory, apart from a wooden desk, a visitors' book and a pen. Outside, the sign for the Virunga National Park was riddled with bullet holes, a reminder that the volcano wasn't the only thing to be wary of. Those bullet holes could have been made by members of any number of militia gangs. And since that first visit, at least four of the rangers protecting the park and animals that I have worked with personally have been killed in the line of duty.

I'd never rigged a volcano before so I hadn't packed light. I'd brought 20 bags of ropes and a big Larkin Rescue Frame, a structure which would allow me to run ropes over the lip of the crater without touching the walls. We'd also hired 100 porters from a local village to help carry our gear up the volcano, as well as the camping kit, medical kit, tons of food and gallons of water. The idea of them helping white people with their exploring seemed rather colonial and made me feel uncomfortable. But there was no other way science or filming could happen there.

At least we were injecting money into the community. We certainly paid them more than they were used to, because they were used to almost nothing.

The Democratic Republic of the Congo is one of the poorest countries in the world, and tougher looking people you never will see. As if the constant banditry, war and poverty wasn't enough, they also have to put up with erupting volcanoes and all sorts of other difficult natural phenomena. Lake Kivu is an 'exploding lake' – the carbon dioxide which seeps from vents around its shore kills a number of locals each year. I couldn't help but notice that the people who live around Goma never seemed to smile, even when you got to know them and they turned out to be friendly. They were wary of foreigners after decades of being colonised and endless violence, and I found myself looking into their dead eyes and wondering what terrible things they'd seen.

It took our group six hours to reach the top, climbing along a tight jungle track and alternating between different biomes. One minute we'd be in dark green alpine montane forest, the next we'd find ourselves in scrub, then in dank cloud forest, with clouds hanging around the canopy of the crooked trees. We were continually shrouded in damp mist, and the higher we got, the colder it became. At one point, massive hailstones started winging in sideways. And the whole time I was on edge, because I imagined men with AK-47s lurking behind every tree.

When we finally reached the peak, what I saw tied my stomach in knots. With everything I'd seen and done in the military, and having planned everything on this trip to the letter, I wasn't expecting to be overawed. But that's how I felt. And dumbstruck.

Looking into that volcano was like looking into a vast eye in the centre of the planet, or a giant cauldron full of the most evil putrid ingredients. Bubbling, whooshing, and looking like it was ready to blow. Just looking at it might have been fine, but I knew I had to lead the filming of a scientific expedition down into the very bowels of it. I was supposed to get a film crew and thousands of pounds' worth of kit inside – my stomach lurched at the prospect.

Everyone was looking at me to make things happen. But I felt like bailing. I wasn't so much scared as angry with myself. I'd been too blasé. It had never entered my head that the job would be this daunting. Being in the Marines had taught me to cope with being out of my comfort zone. Through practice, you can gain enough self-confidence in your ability to deal with danger/risk. So making strong decisions in trying circumstances came with the territory. But this was the first time I'd struggled since leaving the Marines.

I had a massive lump in my throat and negative self-talk was banging around my head: 'I thought I'd done pretty much everything in my life, but I've actually done nothing. What am I doing here?' I decided to take myself off and have a word with myself for five minutes. I needed to calm down and decide what to do.

I asked myself, 'Right, Aldo, what would you tell other people to do in this situation? What is the plan? What needs to be achieved or arranged? What are the hazards and what is needed to mitigate those?' My training kicked in and, once I had assessed the risks and started to think about necessary actions, I was able to feel more in control of the situation and my ability to do what was necessary.

I said to myself, 'How do you write a book? You don't sit down and do it in one go, you write it a page at a time. So just start writing the first page . . .' Dealing with live volcanoes or any dangerous situation requires the same methodical approach.

Having composed myself, I gathered everyone together and got all the kit lined up. Nice and neat. Then I got people to put up their tents. That used up some time, and it was familiar to me. That's what those early stages were about, familiarising myself with the process and recalibrating with the new environment. I was hyper-sensitive because I'd never been there before and I saw danger and problems everywhere. So I broke everything down into little stages, making it into a process. Like a sniper, doing everything in a slow, controlled and methodical way – 'controlling the controllables'. Once I started doing that, I actually started to relax and enjoy myself.

Alex went back down with the porters to take care of some paperwork, leaving me and Mike at the top with three or four armed park rangers. And this great big volcano. Then came night, which was when the volcano really displayed its awesome power. When it's dark, the lava lake resembles the Eye of Sauron from *The Lord of the Rings*. Or the entrance to hell.

The lava lake is an immense circle of roaring molten rock – glowing ferociously and turning everything red: the sky, the clouds and the towering rock walls around it. As it swirls, it creates a disconcerting whooshing sound just as if a giant has poked his stick in there and is stirring those malevolent ingredients. Above us was a towering cloud of gas escaping from the cone, while below us we watched a thunderstorm sending its lightning smashing into Goma. When I finally retreated from the spectacle to my tent, I couldn't sleep for the whooshing, the rumbling and the crashing of falling rocks. It was one of the most exhilarating nights of my life. So far.

The next morning, we started rigging. We were setting up for the TV crew ahead of the arrival of the team of scientists and this process was made a lot easier by the arrival of a couple of French guys (one of whom was the safety man for the famous Brazilian photojournalist Sebastião Salgado). The National Geographic photographer Carsten Peter was coming up later, to take snaps of the scientists for *National Geographic*. That made something click in my mind. I realised, 'If you've got a taste for adventure, there are jobs all over the world. This guy is following a photographer to the ends of the earth. There are all these people doing amazing things in extreme places all over the world and I can be one of them.'

These two French dudes had been inside the volcano before (the rigger was also a volcanologist), which meant Mike and I could watch and learn. They were very relaxed and would bang a piece of rebar (reinforced steel bar) into this crumbly ash ground, tie a rope around it and abseil down. My offshore experience meant I was much more belt and braces. I was also wearing a helmet and goggles and had a gas mask hanging from my neck, so that when the wind changed I wouldn't swallow 'Pele's hair', which are the fine strands of volcanic glass produced by the molten rock (named not after the footballer, but the Hawaiian goddess of volcanoes). Not that any of these precautions made it feel safe, because it was difficult to ignore the giant lava lake creaking and roaring below me.

I attached the anchors and abseiled the first 10 metres, stopping precariously balanced on a tiny razor-sharp ridge of ash, shouting to Mike to start walking down above me. Immediately an ash ledge he stood on crumbled and he lost his footing, sending ash and rocks hurtling towards me. I managed to swing out of the way, but the slack in the line meant that Mike fell five or six metres and smashed hard into the wall beside me. He thought he might have broken his femur, judging by his language. And I couldn't help thinking, 'This is only day one!' Luckily, it turned out his thigh was just badly bruised. Good job, because had he broken it, the whole lot of us would have been on our way back to the UK. This was our first lesson in the level of attention needed to work in this volatile environment.

We spent the best part of a day rigging down to what we called 'Tier 1', which was a flat, rocky section 40 or 50 metres long and about 20 metres wide. Getting down there involved a complicated route of about 15 to 20 abseils, balconies and traverses down, across or up and over hanging rocks the size of a large car or house, often with no protection from the threat of tumbling killer rocks. We knew people had used that route before, but it was my job to re-prove it, check it was still safe and add anchors. We also set up a Larkin Rescue Frame on Tier 1, a metal frame system designed for unstable cliff edges which would allow us to do a straight drop and rescue if we needed to bring someone up from Tier 2 below.

Tier 2 was another substantial ledge about 200 metres wide and covering around three-quarters of the inside wall of the volcano. We reached it with a free drop abseil of 80 metres straight from Tier 1, before navigating an extensive and precarious sloping boulder field down to the flat surface of Tier 2. It was like being on the moon down there, covered in dust like talcum powder, with clumps of Pele's hair, huge rocks that had tumbled down from above and lava bombs – lumps of molten rock ejected from the lava lake – the size of your head. Tier 2 was just 100 metres above the furious lava lake, far too close for comfort.

After three days and an untold number of rope trips to carry all sorts of expedition and support kit into the volcano, the rest of the gang arrived, including an international team of scientists, Carsten Peter and the film crew. The crew included director Nick Jordan, producer Laura Warner, cameraman Rob Franklin and sound recordist Darrell Briggs, who would all play a big part in my journey over the next 10 years and become good friends. With them were 100 more porters – many of them women in beautiful flowing robes, and some pregnant – carrying all the scientific and filming equipment to the top of the volcano, much of it on their heads.

Like my Recce work in the military, Mike and I had gone ahead and secured the area before the rest of our unit had arrived to do their thing. Three volcanologists now ventured inside Nyiragongo to take samples. We got everyone down to Tier 2, then two scientists abseiled down to the very bottom, landing on the bed of solidified lava next to the lava lake. They were an incredible sight in their silver protective suits as we filmed from above, two shiny dots silhouetted against the angry red lava. One guy who declined to go down to the bottom, a very experienced Italian volcanologist called Dario Tedesco, thought these blokes were going to get killed and couldn't get his head around how reckless they were being. Especially when their radios stopped working. But I understood. There are only six lava lakes in the world, and this was the only one of significant size. Being in the belly of Mount Nyiragongo must be the volcanologist's equivalent of playing in a World Cup final for a footballer.

We watched them for a while through binoculars, then saw them suddenly dart down a slope away from the lake, just as a huge wave of lava came sloshing over the rim. If that wave had hit a few seconds earlier, they would have been vaporised. Literally. But they weren't down there for the craic and the thrill of it, they were doing important science, collecting samples and trying to gain a greater understanding of how the volcano worked and when it might erupt again, providing an early warning for the people of Goma.

The most dangerous part of the job was moving the film crew in and out. Those guys weren't experienced on ropes and found themselves suspended over a boiling, hissing lava lake. So having got everyone in and out of the volcano with the necessary footage, back to Goma and then out of the country in one piece, I felt tremendously satisfied. TV's a paradox, and quite illusory, because programme makers want viewers to think they're watching something extremely dangerous, while keeping risk levels to a minimum. All my processes on that trip (apart from going for that daft wander around Goma) had to be double or triple bombproof. I was basically the risk–reward guy, working out how we could get the most epic shots while making sure no one was harmed in the process.

There were so many things that could have gone wrong on that trip, from being kidnapped by rebels to being boiled to death in a lava lake, but everyone got what they wanted and got home safely.

I got what I wanted too. Back home in Scotland, I couldn't quite get over the fact that what I'd done in the Congo was an actual job. Before that trip, it hadn't even crossed my mind that you could get paid for that kind of action in the TV industry. A whole new world had opened up before me. I felt like Lucy from *The Lion, the Witch and the Wardrobe* after returning from Narnia for the first time. I was on cloud nine and my passion for action, adventure and exploring had been rekindled. It was as if I was the 12-year-old me again, getting all giddy about being in the Marines. And if you had told me when I was 16 that I'd be abseiling into an active volcano when I was 32, and getting paid for it, I'd have thought it was just about the perfect job.

I wanted more, and little did I know that I'd be back at Mount Nyiragongo again before long . . .

CHAPTER 6

Extreme, Remote and Hostile:
You Make Your Own Luck

Some people might put my breaking into TV down to luck. If that friend of a friend hadn't happened to mention I worked with ropes, I certainly would never have gone to the Congo.

But I looked at it another way. I was subconsciously making myself available for that kind of opportunity. Everything I'd done up to that point – the skills I'd acquired in the Scouts and the military and on the rigs, obtaining almost every qualification known to man in my spare time, plus all the adventure stuff I'd done for fun – had prepared me for this. I just hadn't known the work existed.

It's important to stress that the journey into Nyiragongo didn't change my life overnight. The wind turbine work carried on because I was still unknown in the world of TV. It was six months before I did my second TV job, which was helping change the lightbulb on Salisbury Cathedral spire – the tallest spire in the UK. That was for the kids' programme *Blue Peter*, with Rob Franklin, the cameraman from the volcano. I was in charge of the ropework, and the presenter Helen Skelton changed the bulb. That was the first time I'd worked with a celebrity, and I was amazed at how normal she was – just another person doing a job.

Shortly after that, Nick Jordan, the director on the Congo job, invited me down to Ripon, North Yorkshire, to take charge of the rigging on another segment for *Richard Hammond's Journey to the Centre of the Planet*, this time about sinkholes. The sinkholes in Ripon are so big they've been known to swallow houses. The one I rigged was said to have inspired Lewis Carroll's *Alice's Adventures in Wonderland*. But I didn't see any Cheshire cats or white rabbits down there, just some old fridges. I ended up doing the filming as well, because the cameraman didn't have the proper insurance to go down. He gave me instructions over the radio and watched on his monitor, while I did a panning shot that ended up being used in the doc. It wasn't quite the Congo, but I loved being involved with all aspects of the filming.

My next TV gig was after another call from Alex and involved rigging for a celebrity *It's a Knockout*-type show in Norway called *71 Degrees North*. I mobilised a team of 10 former Marines to help me with all the rigging and safety. It was a great feeling to be able to offer friends an amazing job that was well-paid and enjoyable. The main thing I remember about that job was how bitterly cold it was. One night we had to bring John Barnes down out of the Portaledge as it was -25°C. When Rob Franklin got in touch again asking if I'd be interested in doing some cave rigging in Slovakia, I realised that getting on in TV is a lot about getting on with people.

In life, people often buy people. That's true in most sectors and businesses, even more so in the TV industry. If you're a bit of a prick, people don't want to work with you. If you cut corners or make the job difficult, you're not going to get a call. There are loads of people out there more qualified at what I do than me, and some viewers probably watch me on TV and think, 'I could have tied that knot better.' But they couldn't – because they weren't there, and I was. And the reason I was there was because the people who hired me knew I'd graft and get on with the job. They knew that when everyone else had gone to bed, I'd stay up another two hours and make sure everything was put away properly, so that when they woke up, it looked like the magic fairy had been. And they knew that while I was safe, I was also amenable. In the Congo, no one knew this bloke who was looking after them, but it was essential that they listened to me and that they trusted me. I quickly realised I was a good communicator in these circumstances, able to relay instructions clearly and put people at ease.

I was also empathetic, understanding that TV people are creatives, wanting to push boundaries. I know that a lot of ex-military would find working with TV people a nightmare. In the military, it's about giving and obeying orders. TV is about compromise. I couldn't just say to the director, 'No. You can't do that or take that shot. That's not going to happen.' I had to say, 'Doing it that way is too dangerous. But there's another way you could do it. The shot might not be quite as good, but nobody will get injured or killed.' I had to come up with solutions, rather than just stonewalling all the time, which effectively meant I became a key part of the creative process. I wasn't going to get upset about a director taking hours over a shot. And instead of saying no, I was going to help make the magic happen, to help them do their job. It reminded me of being in the military. I wasn't the best at any particular thing there, but I grafted and I listened and I took advantage of all the training available. I also got on with people and made myself a key part of any team.

The job in Slovakia was different than everything I'd done so far in that the crew was filming a re-enactment for an American feature documentary. The documentary was based on a memoir called *We Fight to Survive*, by a woman called Esther Stermer.

Stermer was the matriarch of five Ukrainian Jewish families who hid from the Nazis in underground caves for 511 days during the World War Two. The cave in Slovakia doubled for one of those Ukrainian caves, and the scene involved the American caver who stumbled upon the personal effects of those families in the 1990s. The documentary was called *No Place on Earth*, and at the end the director Janet Tobias, someone else who has played a big role in my life, takes some of the survivors, one now a nonagenarian, back to the original caves. That was a hugely memorable job at the start of my TV career.

I'd been working in TV for just over a year but, while I was keeping my ear to the ground, the jobs were still only trickling in. It was going to take time to build my new career. Next was a Channel 4 show called *Hidden Talent*, which involved a famous climber called Leo Houlding, a hero of mine at the time and a good mate now. They matched his bio and psychometrics with 10 volunteers who had never climbed before, and the volunteers took part in a selection weekend to find the most naturally gifted novice climber. The winner was a 45-year-old nurse and grandmother. Within a day, Leo had taught her how to climb and she then went and scaled the Old Man of Stoer, a spectacular 60-metre sandstone sea stack in Sutherland, Scotland.

That show struck a chord with me. If you're from a comfortable background and/or go to a good school, you'll have more opportunities and a far better chance of experiencing different activities and discovering your talents and passions. Many less privileged people go through life not knowing what they're capable of and never reaching their potential, because they're not even aware of the options out there. How many working-class kids know they can be a wildlife camera person, bouncing around the world, seeing amazing things and earning hundreds of pounds a day? Or a documentary producer? Do careers officers go into their schools and tell them? Do they have contacts or know people working in the media who can support and encourage them to explore these careers? I doubt it. And if working-class kids do find out what's out there, they're more likely to think they're not welcome anyway.

I had a bit of an inferiority complex when I was trying to break into expeditions that were run by the military. It seemed to be a closed shop, with mainly graduates and officers being selected. I was mates with a lot of them, but they'd been to good schools and universities, whereas I was a working-class kid from a normal council estate. But when I started working with all these creative types in TV, I realised they were no different to me. The difference was that they just hadn't seen ceilings where others had. They'd aimed high and smashed right through them. My complex was my own doing. People weren't stopping me from achieving, *I* was stopping myself. It's not about being rich or poor, educated or not, it's about understanding that nearly all limits are self-imposed limits. A highly motivated person can accomplish great things and succeed against the odds – another life lesson. I was trying to do the same, showing that anyone, including me, can do anything if they really want to. It's like that Muhammad Ali quote when someone asked if he was any good at golf: 'I'm the best. I just haven't played it yet.' I've never actually thought I was the best at anything, but I'll give pretty much anything a go.

I was a hostile environment safety supervisor on *Driven to Extremes*, a Discovery Channel show that pitted A-list celebrities (Tom Hardy, Henry Cavill and Adrien Brody) and motorsport legends (Superbike racer Neil Hodgson and Formula One driver Mika Salo) against three of the toughest roads on earth. The hottest was through the Taklamakan Desert in China, the wettest was the Ulu Sedili trail through the Malaysian rainforest and the coldest was the Road of Bones in Siberia, so called because so many Soviet prisoners died building it. I spent 10 days with Tom Hardy on that road – not that I knew who he was because I still didn't watch much TV. But that probably worked better because I just treated him like anyone else.

Every job I was offered was through word of mouth and personal recommendation, including the next one, which was a BBC kids' programme called *The Big Climb*. Andy Kirkpatrick is a climber from Yorkshire. His speciality is big wall climbing and this show involved him taking his 13-year-old daughter up El Capitan, a 900-metre slab of granite in Yosemite National Park, California (which I'd always wanted to climb). Andy had heard I was a safe pair of hands, which is exactly what he wanted in the circumstances. I was blown away that he had asked me along as I had always held him in high regard after reading his epic and honest book, *Psychovertical*.

People had told him not to take his daughter up there, and he knew I was super-cautious. I'd got used to saying yes to camera operators and directors, whose instinct it was to take risks, then making their plans safe. Andy's daughter made it to the top, becoming the youngest girl to do so. But more importantly, at least as far as I was concerned, nobody got hurt because I had done my job properly.

While the TV work was picking up pace, I was still keeping the day job ticking over, but it was becoming more and more apparent that my days in the energy industry were numbered. While I was on El Capitan, with my feet dangling over the edge of my Portaledge platform, I took a call from one of my guys about a repair he was doing for me. I was pretending to be on another turbine job, and the whole time I was thinking how uninterested I was in that work. I didn't want to be running a business anymore, putting on a suit and speaking to people from Scottish Power or SSE. I wanted to be doing something I was truly passionate about.

Most of the TV work I did in those first couple of years involved ropes, but I was always looking to add more strings to my bow. It's just that I didn't know the strings existed, just as I hadn't known my bow existed.

In July 2013, I took a job with Nick Jordan in the Frasassi Caves in Italy. That was another Richard Hammond show, and our segment involved taking a NASA astrobiologist down to an underground lake where organisms called extremophiles, which can thrive in the most hostile environments (without sunlight or oxygen), were eating the rock and creating sulphuric acid.

I shouldn't really have done that job, because only a couple of months earlier I'd been badly injured in a skiing accident in France. I was standing on the side of the slope, minding my own business, when a snowboarder came smashing into me, sending me flying. I broke all my left ribs, dislocated my shoulder, broke my shoulder blade and fractured my collarbone in three places. I had to be helicoptered off the mountain and, after a stint in a French hospital, I was wheelchaired on to a plane. The specialist back home said it looked like I'd been hit by a bus. But I didn't dare tell Nick about the accident. The whole time I was down in that cave, I was in agony. I was just desperate not to miss out on any opportunities in TV work.

The underwater cameraman in Italy was a great guy called Johnny Rogers and as soon as I saw him filming in the lake, I thought, 'I need my commercial diving qualifications.' I'd been recreational diving for years, in places like Bali and the Philippines, but it had never occurred to me that I might be able to make a living out of it. As soon as I got back from Italy, I booked myself on some courses and earned my commercial scuba diving certificate.

Johnny was a normal lad from Ardglass, County Down – just getting on with things, having lots of fun and making good money. For Johnny, his job wasn't just a job, it was a lifestyle, a way of living. I could see myself in Johnny, and he had a big influence on me. Johnny told me that there were only two places to be if you wanted a career like his – London or Bristol, where the BBC Natural History Unit is based. So Bristol was where I moved to in November 2013. I also had a website built and started my own company, called Vertical Planet. Looking back, meeting Johnny in Italy was a tipping point. There was no going back after that. Wind turbines were almost in the past, TV was my future.

I already knew quite a few people in Bristol, through the various TV jobs I'd done. So shortly after moving down there, I arranged a night out. It was a little odd, in that most people knew each other but they might not have necessarily hung out together. And some people didn't even know who had organised it because they'd been invited second-hand. I spent the night chatting to everyone and handing out my business card. It was about letting people know I existed and making contacts. I knew the work was there and I needed to push myself into that world to create a steady income.

The following year, 2014, was a whirlwind. One week I was on top of a 35-metre chimney in Burton-on-Trent, the next I was up a transmitting station in Yorkshire, then I was in the Gomantong Cave in Borneo. My last wind turbine job was that summer. Instead of cleaning up oil inside a giant metal tube, I would be working on a Hollywood blockbuster next.

Almost every gig I got seemed to take me in a new direction. A cameraman I'd worked with previously just happened to be moving into feature films, and he got me a job working on *In the Heart of the Sea*, directed by the legendary Ron Howard (*A Beautiful Mind*) and starring Chris Hemsworth. *In the Heart of the Sea* was about the sinking of the American whaling ship *Essex* in 1820, which inspired Herman Melville's *Moby-Dick*. I spent four or five weeks in a studio in Hertfordshire as part of the grips team in charge of lighting and rigging, standing in a lookout that doubled as a ship's mast, pulling ropes, working pulleys and moving cameras around.

While I was there, I found myself watching the stunt team and thinking, 'Why can't I do that instead?' Stunt rigging was yet another thing I didn't know existed, and I soon learned that stunt riggers didn't even need any special qualifications. So I did what I always do, I made myself busy, worked hard and spoke to as many people as possible. A couple of months later, I rigged a stunt for the Scottish trials cyclist Danny MacAskill, which involved him jumping off a crane in Glasgow for the opening of the Commonwealth Games in 2014. Shortly after that I got a call from someone asking if I wanted to work on the new Avengers movie, *Age of Ultron*.

Put simply, stunt riggers are people who make stunts happen. For example, if someone gets shot in a movie, they might have a harness on which is attached to a rope, which some stunt riggers will pull to make it look like they've been blown off their feet by the force of the bullet. And on *Age of Ultron*, we made Chris Hemsworth, who was playing Thor, fly from one end of a tanker to the other, before landing on deck and smashing up a load of baddies with his hammer.

Age of Ultron was an all-star cast – Hemsworth, Mark Ruffalo,

Chris Evans, Scarlett Johansson and many others – which makes it sound very glamorous, but it's not as if I was hanging out with them after work. I was driving from Bristol to Hertfordshire almost every day for two-and-a-half months, and when I got there, I didn't actually do much, even though the pay was great. The process of filmmaking is excruciatingly slow, with each piece of action covered in loads of different ways. I was a tiny cog in this giant machine – but I was constantly watching and learning and making contacts. It was better than cleaning wind turbines, but it was nothing like as exciting as being in a volcano.

If it sounds like the transition from old life to new life was plain sailing, it wasn't. There are many disadvantages and downsides to an adventurous life that aren't plastered all over social media, and one is that your home life can be chaotic and fractured, as I was finding out. I'd met my fiancée six years earlier in 2007, when I was out of the Marines and working offshore. She was originally from the Cotswolds and had been pushing for a move down south for a while, so when I told her I wouldn't mind moving to Bristol, she was over the moon.

Looking back, it was selfish on my part. She wanted to be in Bristol to be near her family, but I wanted to be there to further my TV health and safety career. She'd been used to me being away for two weeks at a time on the rigs, but found the TV gigs more problematic. Cracks had started to appear in our relationship even before the move, but now I might be away for months and when I got back, I'd have to fix a wind turbine or would be off climbing or skiing or to get another qualification.

It was difficult as we loved each other, but my other passion was taking me further and further away from home. I desperately needed the adventure.

When someone called, asking me if I wanted to drive across Siberia with Tom Hardy, I'd be elated. But when I got home, I wouldn't mention it. Climbing El Capitan had been a dream of mine for years, but I couldn't share the experience with her. Even mentioning it felt selfish. It reached the stage where I'd keep things to myself, so that I was almost leading a double life. I could see that it was a train wreck waiting to happen, but I was too cowardly to stop it. Eventually she asked me if I was ever going to stop doing 'that kind of work'.

People think I'm brave, but there are different kinds of courage. Facing ridiculous physical challenges was fun, but when I needed to make a tough decision for both of us, I avoided it.

If my fiancée thought I might change my ways, 2014 must have been a big disappointment for her. We got married that October, and I knew that my choices would be even more difficult to accept now that I was her husband. She told me that I needed to spend more time at home. A few weeks later, I left for an incredible opportunity to work on a documentary about the Ebola outbreak in Africa. I ran away, trying to ignore that part of my life that was creaking, crumbling and about to collapse. The truth was that I really wanted to take that job, and I was going to have to live with the sacrifices necessary for the life I had chosen.

CHAPTER 7

Unseen Enemy: Life is Fragile

I'd been married for only a couple of weeks when Janet Tobias, who I'd worked with in Slovakia and who had become a good friend, phoned and said, 'Do you want to work for me in Africa again?'

I'd already led an expedition to the Congo earlier that year, for a film about the threat of pandemics in the twenty-first century. *Unseen Enemy* was directed by Janet and the focus of the segment was a Belgian microbiologist called Peter Piot, who helped discover the Ebola virus in what was then Zaire in 1976. Piot, now the director of the London School of Hygiene and Tropical Medicine, described its origins and how it had wiped out almost the entire village of Yambuku (the virus had an 88% mortality rate back then), which is near the Ebola River, deep in the Congolese rainforest.

Reaching Yambuku had taken us several days by plane, 4x4 and eventually foot, hacking through the jungle with machetes. We finally came to an abandoned settlement, almost completely reclaimed by the forest. After several hours of clearing the site with our machetes, we found ourselves standing at the foot of three crumbling gravestones. Buried beneath them were the bodies of three Belgian nuns, who were from Yambuku's Catholic mission and among the first to die in the outbreak. Peter recalled that when he'd first arrived in the village in 1976, a nun had appeared and shouted, 'Don't come any nearer! Stay outside the barrier or you will die just like us!' Nine of 17 hospital staff had died, as had 39 of 60 people living in the mission, plus four nuns and two priests.

I hadn't expected to hear anything about Ebola again, but shortly after getting home, news broke about an outbreak in several West African countries. The media were hyping up the outbreak, as they usually do, making it sound like the end of the world. So when I had the call, my family and friends were telling me not to go, because I might die. But I trusted Janet. I'd also be working with Pulitzer Prize-winning journalist Laurie Garrett, who had been in lots of pandemic hotspots and written a book about the 1995 Ebola outbreak in the Congo, plus illustrious cinematographer César Charlone, who worked on the classic Brazilian film *City of God*. It was impossible to say no.

While I'd be lying if I said I wasn't attracted by the adventure – going somewhere new and dangerous where I'd be living by my wits – I also thought it would be a worthy thing to do. A team was going with or without me, so if I could make sure they stayed safe and managed to get an important story out into the wider world, I'd have done something good. As with anything like that, it was about weighing up the risks and the rewards. Not that my wife agreed.

Despite the reassurances from Janet and Peter Piot, my nerves were jangling on the flight from Brussels to the Liberian capital of Monrovia. I was acutely aware of how tightly packed the plane was and of every cough or sneeze. To calm myself down, I had to think back to my experience.

When I was in the Marines, people were always telling you, 'If you fuck this up, you'll die.' That's why they drill you relentlessly, so you don't. By the time I'd got on that plane, I'd been through the risk assessment in my head a thousand times. Ebola was moving through West Africa fast and people were dying on the streets. But I also knew it was transmitted by infected blood and bodily fluids and I'd only catch it by being careless. It wasn't much different to the coronavirus situation: I had to keep my distance, not touch anyone or anything, wear personal protective equipment (PPE) and wash my hands regularly. I don't think I touched my face once during that flight. Not because I thought there was Ebola on the plane, but as an exercise in discipline.

I was to spend the first couple of weeks with Laurie, in charge of security, as well as laying the groundwork for the arrival of Janet and César as location producer and helping secure contacts and leads. Laurie was an American journalist straight out of central casting: loud and abrasive. Given that I was supposed to be looking after her, she seemed like a handful. But I was also in awe of her. She'd spent so much time in places other reporters wouldn't have touched in order to tell the world about deadly diseases like Ebola, SARS and avian flu. As a senior fellow of the Council on Foreign Relations, she reported directly to the Pentagon about how and why these viruses were spreading. And she was finding things out and getting things done even before the plane had landed in Monrovia.

Our fixer, Nuru, was a tall, smiley man with haunted eyes. You could tell he'd been through a lot. He was a local reporter and our eyes and ears, the man who knew where and who everyone was. He'd tell us where we could and couldn't go, who we could and couldn't speak to, what we could and couldn't say. In turn, Nuru had his own stringers, dotted all over the country. Our driver was called Gabriel and looked like he hadn't slept for weeks. Drivers and fixers are the unsung heroes of documentary making, the people who open doors and make things happen.

It's no exaggeration to say that no films would ever get made in developing countries without their help.

The morning after our arrival, Gabriel drove us to West Point, one of the poorest neighbourhoods in Monrovia and scene of a recent 21-day lockdown. West Point is situated on a slither of land surrounded by water and has one road in and out. So when government officials locked the gate, no one could leave. Shortly before our arrival, the police had shot a kid because he'd tried to escape, and there was a lot of resentment bubbling under the surface.

West Point is a densely populated labyrinth, consisting of a long, narrow street flanked by market stalls, surrounded for miles by shacks with corrugated iron roofs. My first thought was, 'If anything kicks off here, there's nowhere to escape to.' Not that Laurie seemed in the slightest bit concerned. Nuru had to keep reminding her not to take any photos, because many locals were convinced that white folk made money out of them. And she seemed perplexed as to why I was there. Was I her minder? Her medic? Her general dogsbody? She had a point. She'd seen more action than most soldiers I knew.

We'd only been in West Point for 20 minutes when we came to a Red Cross ambulance blocking the road. Emergency workers in full biohazard suits were hosing someone down with chlorine solution, and a body had just been recovered from the labyrinth. It was like a scene from seventeenth-century London during the plague. In the summer it had been far worse, with bodies stacked up on the streets. But my biggest concern wasn't catching Ebola on the streets, it was being involved in a road accident and catching it in hospital. That's why I carried a trauma bag, containing everything from airways to tourniquets to drugs to surgical kit.

Laurie had heard that a local archbishop had been telling people that Ebola was God's punishment for homosexuality, so we headed to Nuru's local church to see if the rumours were true. Before entering Bethel Cathedral of Hope, we washed our hands from a bucket of running chlorinated water and had our temperature taken. Inside, there must have been 600 worshipers, wearing every colour of the rainbow. There was a gospel choir behind the preacher, who implored the congregation to 'be strong'. I'm not a religious man, but I found the service moving and uplifting. However, it was also highly problematic. Members of the congregation were dancing and touching hands, and all that loud singing meant lots of open mouths and flying spittle. That's not an ideal combination in a confined space in the middle of a pandemic – as we all now know. It was a deeply paradoxical situation: a gathering of people gaining strength from their faith, while exposing themselves to this terrible disease.

My first visit to an Ebola treatment unit with live cases, run by Médecins Sans Frontières (MSF), was a harrowing experience. On arrival, we were given a briefing, which mainly consisted of the liaison officer telling us not to touch anything and disinfect our hands if we did. We slipped into wellington boots, which were then disinfected, before washing our hands in chlorine solution. When Laurie dropped her pen and went to pick it up, everything went in slow time. I half expected a doctor to shout 'NOOOO!' and throw their body on top of it, as if it was a grenade.

The unit had strict processes in place. New arrivals were sifted and tested, before being sent off to separate compounds: probable, confirmed and convalescing. We were led to three large tents. In these tents, staff worked eight-hour shifts while wearing

PPE in the sweltering temperatures. And after every shift, they had to carry out a 32-stage decontamination process before they were allowed to leave. These people truly were on the frontline of a battle.

The doctor told us that the people we could see outside the tents were getting better, but those inside were dying. Some of those who had survived remained in the unit to help out. Most of them had nowhere else to go, because they'd been ostracised by their families. Some helpers had never spent any time in the unit as a patient, but their communities had cast them out after their families had died. Their stories were terribly sad, but their presence gave hope to the suffering, because it showed Ebola could be beaten. The fact that they didn't wear masks also provided the patients with a slither of intimacy, because everyone else was hidden inside a yellow biohazard suit.

In the diagnostics tent, a man in his thirties was being sprayed down by three people in biohazard suits. We were only a few metres away from him, behind a waist-high barrier. Close enough to feel his terror. The poor bloke had just buried his wife, who had died of Ebola, and was now feeling sick. After he was led away to have his blood taken, we didn't expect to see him again.

On the way out, I noticed a wooden board hanging on the wall which was covered in handprints – the handprints of the survivors, the few. It was a makeshift board of white chipboard and each print was a story of survival against all odds. The prints came in every colour – pink, blue, orange, red and more – and as the weeks and months passed, the board was extended and new prints were added. This was a choking and heartwarming sight at the same time. There was some hope, after all, for the patients and those on the frontline of the fight.

That visit was a sobering experience, but people were keen to assure us that things had improved significantly. At a brand-new Ministry of Defence unit, the doctor in charge was a Liberian called Soka Moses. At the start of the outbreak, Dr Moses had set up the JFK Hospital, which was a bunch of shacks, tents and blue tarpaulin. There were so many patients and so few beds that the nurses barely had space to walk between them. About half of those admitted to the unit died. And dying from Ebola is hideous. Ebola is a viral haemorrhagic fever, which means a victim loses all the fluids from their body. In the tents for the dying, naked victims would lie on beds with no sheets. The beds would be attached to funnels, through which the bodily fluids would run away.

Dr Moses was only two years out of medical school when the crisis hit and had read only one paper on Ebola before he set up the JFK Hospital. He was one of only a few dozen Liberian doctors in a country of just under five million people. Some of those doctors had died, as had a few of Dr Moses' nurses.

We also got to visit the American unit, built by the US Agency for International Development (USAID) and the US Public Health Service (USPHS), which was altogether different. For a start, it only treated healthcare workers who had contracted the virus through the line of duty. The unit was an air-conditioned labyrinth of neat military tents. The shelves were stacked with PPE, every bed had its own monitoring kit and every patient received IV therapy. I only saw it before it opened and have no idea if it was ever used. It all seemed slightly unfair when Liberians were dying under tin roofs. But it was where I wanted to go if I ever got Ebola.

After a few days, it became clear that I wasn't just Laurie's security, I was also an extra fixer: negotiating, sorting out paperwork, hustling flights. As the trip wore on, I'd also become a location producer and investigative journalist, following leads, getting stories, sending daily briefs back to Janet in America.

I managed to get me and Laurie on a humanitarian aid plane up to Sierra Leone, because none of the civilian carriers were travelling between the affected countries. While Liberia seemed to have the virus under control, in Sierra Leone it was said to be spreading nine times faster than two months earlier. Laurie's plan was to get out of the Sierra Leone capital Freetown as soon as possible and head down to the border with Liberia, which was experiencing a particularly sharp spike in infections. Her hunch was that the virus was being carried over the border by the migration of people, even though the border was supposed to be locked down.

Laurie was now on a mission, like Martin Sheen in *Apocalypse Now*, and I was being dragged along with her. I'd been on missions before, but this was a particularly mad one. Not only were we planning to travel right into the heart of an Ebola hotspot, where our unseen enemy could be lurking on every surface, but Sierra Leone was a very dangerous place anyway, minus the virus.

It soon became apparent that Sierra Leone was nothing like as wise to the virus as Liberia. The finger scanner at the airport wasn't cleaned after each use. The ferry port, from where we caught a taxi across the river to Freetown, was rammed. When I told our fixer I needed to buy a couple of sim cards, I was quickly surrounded by hawkers, pushing sim cards into my hands.

The Connaught Hospital in Freetown was a normal hospital trying to function as an Ebola treatment unit. In front of the main entrance was the screening unit, which was a rickety wooden shelter. And a few metres away from that was a shelter for suspected Ebola sufferers, open on all sides and surrounded by what appeared to be bodily fluid stains on the tarmac. An English doctor explained that the four people in that shelter were waiting for a bed, and that most of them would die before one became available. These doctors and nurses were doing everything they could to save people, but it still wasn't good enough.

On the way to Kerry Town, we stopped off at a small treatment unit just off a dirt road in a town called Hastings. In Liberia, we would have been stopped at the front gate and hosed down with bleach. But in this case, we walked straight in, with me filming on a GoPro camera. Once inside, Laurie bowled through a crowd as if it didn't exist and straight into an office, where some Cuban doctors were being briefed. It was a Sierra Leonean military unit and the chief doctor seemed only too happy to give us a guided tour.

I flashed a business card from the deputy minister for health and the boss immediately gave me permission to film his staff inside the red zone, where the infected patients were, using the GoPro. Part of me was hoping the head nurse, Justice, would put the kybosh on our plans, and my heart sank a bit when he readily agreed.

The unit had lost several workers in the last couple of months, so I used my own PPE, including a bright yellow XL biohazard suit for extra breathing space. I got ready with the other nurses, following the same strict procedure – suit on first, then gloves, then mask, then goggles, then hairnet. Then I put my hood up and taped the suit, before pulling on a second set of gloves, taping up my wrists and dunking my GoPro in chlorine solution. As a finishing touch, someone wrote my name on my apron in blue marker pen. I was used to feeling this claustrophobic, having done plenty of diving, and I had worn a biohazard suit (an NBC suit – nuclear, biological and chemical suit) when being bombed in Iraq. But despite looking utterly impregnable, I felt terribly anxious.

Someone lifted the tarpaulin and opened the door, and I followed the nurses into the red zone, filming as I went. In the first room, the male ward, were three patients, surrounded by nine empty beds and not much else. The nurses started changing a patient's cannula, which was something I knew how to do. But I'd never done it in full PPE, while feeling like I was slowly boiling in a bag. When the needle went in, some blood dripped down the patient's arm and onto the floor. In slow-motion, like in a movie. It was only a drop, but deadly.

Two of the patients appeared stable, the other didn't. A middle-aged man, he was lying on his side on the bare plastic mattress, which was covered in diarrhoea and vomit. Ebola sufferers can evacuate up to 12 litres of bodily fluids a day. Like most of the patients, he was naked, because not being so would have meant his clothing being infected. While the nurses were treating the other patient, the man started writhing around before falling on the floor with a thump. As the nurses lifted him back onto the bed, all he could see were their eyes behind thick goggles. The poor guy must have been so scared. Those goggle-encased eyes would probably be his last glimpse of humanity.

It was a similar sight in the women's ward, naked patients lying in their own excrement and vomit, which also covered the tiled floor. As Justice attempted to cannulate a young woman, she looked straight into my eyes. She was clearly petrified and in tremendous pain. Justice tried three times to drive the needle into her arm but couldn't locate a vein. By now, my knees were weak, my breathing was heavy, my goggles were so foggy I could barely see through them and my boots were full of sweat in the fierce heat. Justice felt for another vein further up the patient's arm. Her eyes told me she knew this was the difference between life and death, but there was nothing she could do to help herself.

Justice missed a vein again. I briefly caught his eye. This wasn't what he wanted me to see. As Justice withdrew the needle, the tape on the patient's arm snagged his glove and tore a small hole. I pointed to Justice's finger and he plunged his hand into a bucket of chlorine solution. Luckily, the tape had only torn his outer glove. I could almost hear my heart pounding. I was half breathing, half gasping. Justice removed his outer gloves, snapped on a new pair and began the process again. He tightened the tourniquet, making the veins in her arm pop. And this time, the needle found its mark.

After an hour in the red zone I was physically and mentally spent, as if I had just climbed El Capitan or fought my way out of an ambush in Iraq. And I'd only been watching for one hour. The doctors and nurses at Hastings often did eight-hour shifts in the red zone.

I signalled to Justice that I'd seen enough. But the most dangerous part of the mission was still to come. In the doffing station, I was met by a supervisor who told me to stop and spread my arms and legs. He then sprayed me from head to toe with chlorine solution, which stung my eyes as it penetrated the rim of my mask. At the next station, I stepped into a bucket of chlorinated water and rinsed my outer gloves, before the supervisor shouted at me to remove my outer gloves and throw them in a bin. Just removing my suit involved something like 10 stages, plus hand washing after every one of them.

I was fairly certain I was the first 'journalist' to enter an Ebola treatment unit red zone. And I suppose I could now call myself a camera operator, on top of everything else. They say the best journalists are empathetic, but I cared so much for these Ebola sufferers that I sometimes felt like I shouldn't be there. Intruding on grief, asking awkward questions, then walking away.

While it was probably the best unit we visited, the British Army officers attached to it, as with elsewhere in Sierra Leone, didn't seem to understand what was going on with Ebola in the rest of the country. That was one reason Sierra Leone seemed to be so far behind Liberia in terms of its response to the virus. Another reason was corruption. I was told the virus was out of control in Sierra Leone because some rural districts were paying laboratories to lose or lie about positive results, so as not to look bad. I'd also heard that people in rural areas remained convinced that Ebola was the result of witchcraft, while an American preacher had been doing radio interviews in which he claimed the virus had been started by white people, in order to control the African population. In some West African communities, the people thought Ebola didn't exist at all. In one Guinean village, eight members of a team of healthcare workers, journalists and government officials, who had visited to warn about the dangers of Ebola, were massacred.

I witnessed the delicate process of trying to convince rural communities Ebola was real in Liberia. In one bustling settlement about an hour's drive from Monrovia, we filmed a meeting involving representatives from an aid organisation and village chiefs from the area. The chief of chiefs, dressed in ceremonial garb, was drummed into the hall before holding court for about an hour, talking in tribal tongue to his fellow elders. By the end of his speech, everyone seemed to be on board with his message: Ebola is real, it can easily kill you and these people are here to help. Other chiefs might have been as charismatic and persuasive, but they weren't as forward-thinking as this one.

As well as the fake news that was flying all over the place, causing more deaths and making it more difficult to help, politicians were squabbling, money was going missing and new vehicles and entire container loads of PPE were being pinched, before reappearing on the black market. An aid worker told me the Sierra Leonean government wasn't interested in eradicating Ebola, because as long the virus was there, money would keep flowing in. And as long as money kept flowing in, people would keep taking it for themselves.

I'd find myself thinking, 'At least if a pandemic ever arrived in the UK, it would be nothing like this. People would obey orders, stay inside and keep their distance. The government would be on top of it, there wouldn't be any of the lies and corruption you get in developing countries. And everyone would believe it existed and it wasn't a sick hoax.' I was young and naïve, because when coronavirus hit the UK, it wasn't much different.

While Ebola was far worse than coronavirus, the people in those countries had no choice but to get on with their normal lives, just as people got on with their normal lives when I was fighting a war in Iraq. The government wasn't going to give them money, so they had to earn money to buy rice, or they and their family would starve to death. That was the simple equation. (In Liberia they have a saying: 'No rice for lazy man.')

When we flew back to Monrovia, the atmosphere had changed. On the road back to the hotel, police were using batons to control an unruly mob. Nuru explained that people were upset that elections had been postponed. Not that Laurie seemed at all fazed. When we arrived at the Ministry of Health later that day, we found another angry mob of government workers outside. Once inside, I started formulating a plan of escape. Where are the exits? What do we do if any of us get caught? I was relaying my thoughts to the local cameraman we were working with when I looked out of the window and saw Laurie marching into the middle of the mob while scribbling notes.

I ran downstairs, shouldered my way into the middle of the scrum and asked if Laurie was okay. She handed me her scarf and handbag and carried on asking questions.

I'd spent my entire working life, whether in the Marines or out on the oil rigs, trying to be as safe as possible. That meant not taking unnecessary risks. So I found Laurie very difficult to get my head around. I'd remind her of the little things that would pay dividends in keeping her safe – the absolute basics – and she'd roll her eyes and sigh. I'd think, 'Jesus, I'm just trying to make sure you don't die.' And now she'd wandered into the middle of an angry mob of Liberians, and she had no idea what they were angry about. For all she knew, they might have been demanding the expulsion of all Americans. But when Laurie re-emerged from that scrum, she had an important story.

Those workers, who were in their early twenties, had been doing the very dangerous job of keeping tabs on every person in Monrovia who had come into contact with someone with Ebola (contact tracers). They'd been rapping on countless doors, going into countless homes and conducting countless interviews, and they hadn't been paid for two months. That's when I started to understand what proper journalism was all about: most journalists would have swerved that mob, but Laurie dived right in. For all her brashness, she was an incredible journalist doing essential work, getting important stories out to the West. I was blown away by how ballsy she was, how she viewed her responsibility as a journalist as more important than her safety.

For all my vigilance, the only time I really felt in any real danger was when I was wired $2,000 by Janet's production team and had to withdraw it from a Western Union on the outskirts of Freetown. Outside were about 30 soldiers standing around, with AKs hanging from their shoulders. They seemed quite relaxed, but when I went inside, there must have been a hundred more of them, looking pretty pissed off. I later learned they hadn't been paid for three months. I filled out the paperwork and the woman behind the counter said to me, 'Have you got any bags?' Bags. Plural. That's when it suddenly occurred to me that $2,000 in Sierra Leonean leones is a lot of notes.

I went back to the car, grabbed a couple of daysacks, walked back in and started filling the daysacks with the money. The place was suddenly deathly quiet. I could feel the eyes of these angry soldiers drilling a hole in the back of my head and there was sweat running into the crack of my arse. But the scariest part was turning round and leaving. I wouldn't have blamed them had they turned on me: here was this white bloke wandering around with sacks of cash, and they were struggling to feed their families. When I got back in the car, I told the fixer to step on it and we left the soldiers for dust.

After a couple of weeks, Laurie flew back to New York and a cameraman arrived in Monrovia to start filming for Janet's documentary. Dennis' first venue was the MSF unit I'd visited with Laurie 10 days earlier, where five patients were due to be discharged. When we arrived, there seemed to be fewer people in the unit than before and I discerned a buzz of excitement about the place, because everyone knew this was a rare happy day.

The unit's so-called red zone had two exits: one for survivors, one for the dead. Mercifully, we didn't see any body bags that afternoon. The survivors removed their clothes, which were then taken away and incinerated, before a couple of nurses in full PPE poured buckets of chlorinated water over them. They were handed a small towel with which to dry themselves and a new set of clothes, consisting of T-shirt, pants, jeans and flip-flops, after which the tarpaulin was pulled aside and they appeared, with nervous smiles on their faces. They were among the lucky ones, and they were only too aware of it.

They were painfully thin and unsteady on their feet, and just about able to reach a line of seats, where a psychologist chatted to them, to make sure they were okay. The survivors looked dazed, as if they'd just emerged from a cave. Hardly surprising, given that this was the first proper human contact they'd had for weeks. Some of the doctors even shook their hands.

Suddenly, one of the survivors looked over and said weakly, 'I recognise you. How's it going, man?' This was the guy I'd seen being admitted, the one whose wife had died of Ebola, who I thought I'd never see again. Watching him make his handprint on the wooden board was such a beautiful moment to witness. When I asked what he was doing next, he said he hoped to be back at work in the morning. With that, he said goodbye and wandered out of the main gate.

I wondered if the guy's workmates would accept him back into the fold or if he'd be stigmatised and ostracised. That was the fate of many survivors when they returned to their communities, as well as healthcare workers who had never even contracted Ebola, people who should have been greeted as heroes. We spent one afternoon filming a survivors' club meeting, set up by MSF, and the anger and bitterness were obvious. And when we visited a UNICEF care centre for children in Monrovia, I wondered if those kids would be the same when they grew up, rejected by society for something over which they had no control.

Either these kids' parents had died of Ebola or they'd been in contact with an Ebola sufferer in their community, and they'd come to the centre for 21 days' quarantine. There were about 15 kids in all, ranging from six-month-old babies to teenagers. Decontee, a survivor who ran the centre, was only 23. If anyone in the centre started showing Ebola symptoms, they'd be sent to a treatment centre. If they didn't, they'd be sent back home. Whether anyone would want them was anyone's guess. Some of the kids were on their own, the luckier ones had siblings, including one lovely little guy called Morris, who was only six. Morris and his sister had lost their parents the previous week.

In a country like Liberia, where civil wars raged between 1989 and 2003 killing 250,000 people (8% of the population), displacing many more and shrinking the economy by 90%, people had barely got back on their feet before Ebola hit. To them, seemingly monumental events are just things that happen. As long as you don't die, you just carry on as normal. At least that's what it felt like. One day, our fixer Nuru just happened to mention that his wife was having a caesarean section that night. I couldn't believe it. He'd been with us for over two weeks and hadn't once mentioned that his wife was expecting a baby at any moment. Nuru had one day off for a family celebration and was back at work the next day.

A couple of days later, things got even worse when I was denied access to a treatment centre because my temperature was too high. I tried to be rational: I'd been sitting in a hot car for hours. Or maybe it was the thermometer? They were cheap imports from China and maybe weren't calibrated properly. But what if

I suddenly deteriorated and ended up in a local hospital? If I didn't have Ebola before, I'd definitely get it then. If anyone was showing any symptoms, our plan was to take them to the American treatment unit. But I was the one making the plans, so who knew if they'd be followed.

After 20 minutes of waiting outside the centre, I had my temperature tested again and it was now okay. But the following day, I was turned away from another treatment unit and still felt terrible. Janet had now joined us, plus César Charlone, who was getting all sorts of incredible footage, and they and the rest of the crew were aware I'd been knocked back from a couple of units. I decided to isolate in my hotel room for 24 hours, while popping Cipro pills like Pac-Man.

Later that day I felt like death warmed up. I had terrible stomach cramps, my guts were in tatters (I won't go into details) and I was well aware that diarrhoea was one of the main symptoms of Ebola, because it was written on walls wherever we went. That was a rough old night. When I wasn't sitting on the toilet, I had my head down it. And when I wasn't in the bathroom, I was lying on my bed, staring at the ceiling, sweating, clutching my stomach, wondering if I was dying. I had to deal with the facts. And the fact was, I'd spent the last month filming in Ebola treatment centres and now I had diarrhoea and was being sick. All signs pointed to the virus.

I did a lot of thinking that night. I reflected on my time in a war zone, where I was able to see and hear the enemy and take my shots. But in the midst of a pandemic, the enemy is invisible. You don't know who's got Ebola or which inanimate objects it's lurking on. I thought I'd been careful, but also wondered if I'd become complacent and let my guard down. I wracked my brain, trying to remember all my interactions over the previous few days. Had I opened a door for someone without wearing gloves? Had I washed my hands after picking up that bread and water from the shop?

I kept telling myself, 'It could be a million other things, don't let your imagination run riot.' But at about 3am, I started googling Ebola symptoms, which is never a clever thing to do. Yes, it could have been Ebola. But it could also have been dengue fever, from when we'd been out in the bush. Or maybe my malaria tablets weren't working? I fished out my medical book and started reading about all the different gastro issues you can get on your travels. From what the book said, I seemed to have some sort of bacterial issue, possibly caused by a warm sandwich I'd grabbed at the hotel the previous afternoon. So I popped some more Cipro pills, crossed my fingers and finally drifted off to sleep.

I kept clinging to the belief that if I had Ebola, I'd feel significantly worse, which was a strange kind of comfort. And midway through my quarantine, everything started to calm down, gutswise. The morning of my re-emergence, I felt right as rain. The moral of that story? Never eat a warm sandwich in the middle of a pandemic. You might not die of food poisoning, but you might die of fear.

Every day on that trip, I witnessed amazing people doing heroic things despite the danger. One ambulance station was manned by an American guy called Zac. He picked up Ebola sufferers all over Monrovia and ferried them to treatment units. But as well as the ambulance driver, Zac was also a hygienist and counsellor.

We rode with Zac to a job, filming as we went. On the way, the car in front of us hit an old man. He was writhing around and screaming in agony. But instead of stopping, Zac got on the loudspeaker and informed the old man that another ambulance was on the way. Emergency workers in Liberia had to make that kind of snap decision every day during the Ebola crisis. That old man might have broken his leg, but the person we were racing to was dying.

Another day, we went out with a Red Cross body collection team. We rolled out from the compound in a convoy of six SUVs, plus a pickup for the bodies. We weaved our way through tiny dirt streets before reaching a more built-up area, where a crowd of people were staring at a house on a corner. In most communities, the locals were terrified of the virus and wanted the body taken away as soon as possible. The Red Cross counsellor jumped out of an SUV and spoke to the family, before sending the rest of the team in.

One man in full PPE entered the house, spraying chlorine solution as he went. Inside, he took a swab from the dead person's mouth, before emerging and being hosed down with chlorine himself. The body bag team formed a circle, bowed their heads, said a short prayer and bumped fists, before disappearing into the house. While they were inside, triple-bagging the body, the grieving family wailed. Ten minutes later, two of the team appeared in the doorway with a stretcher, carrying the body. At that point, more people started to wail and the atmosphere turned a bit uneasy. Then the stretcher bearers lifted the body onto the truck and dropped it down, rather unceremoniously.

It took about half an hour for the body bag team to remove their PPE, with every stage carefully monitored and supervised. The sloppy removal of PPE was the main cause of death among healthcare workers. The process involved so many steps, and when you've just come off a long shift feeling drained and disorientated from boiling in a biohazard suit for hours, it's easy to make a mistake and get some blood or mucus on your skin.

Even experienced healthcare workers slipped up. And even if they hadn't, they were haunted by the fear that they had. Dr Moses, the guy who set up the JFK Hospital in Monrovia, told me about the time he thought he'd caught Ebola. Dr Moses had been slogging away at JFK, away from his family, because he couldn't risk going home. He'd been changing cannulas, taking blood and removing his PPE while drop-down tired. And after six months, his first nurse died of Ebola. That evening, Dr Moses stopped his car and started weeping, because the gravity of his situation had suddenly dawned on him. One ever so slightly torn glove, one misdirected needle, one small misstep during the PPE removal process, and he might be dead too.

The virus meant that hundreds of years of funeral traditions involving bodies being cleaned and decorated were outlawed, which didn't go down well. Hardly surprising, when strange men in biohazard suits were walking into people's homes, putting their loved ones in plastic bags, dumping them on pick-up trucks and whisking them away, never to be seen again. Many communities ignored the new guidelines, so Ebola outbreaks after funerals were common. Even when a body was in the ground, it remained highly contagious, its fluids often seeping into the water supply.

While burials were officially banned in Liberia in favour of cremation, in Sierra Leone they were still taking place on an industrial scale.

What Janet and the crew understood more than me, being professional journalists, was that if we weren't there, then who else would be telling these stories? Stories that people needed to see, and stories that would hopefully prevent things like this happening in the future. They didn't care any less than me – Janet is one of the most caring people I know – but they knew time was of the essence and were good at compartmentalising things. I thought about things too much, while they understood that thinking too much helps no one.

Sometimes on that trip, I felt like a ghost, wandering through other people's misery, unable to help or even touch anything. In fact, Ebola had turned the entire region into ghosts. I heard so many stories about people dying on the side of the road or giving birth right outside the main entrance of a maternity ward. For me, it felt like being back in Iraq. I was present but I wasn't. It was a surreal experience.

Shortly before leaving Africa for good, we paid a visit to Monrovia's crematorium. Before the Ebola crisis, cremation was alien to most Liberian people. Indeed, when Monrovia's Indian crematorium was first built, it had one altar. But by the time we visited, it was burning 100 bodies a night in British-donated incinerators. The poor blokes working there hadn't been paid for months and were doing one of the most dangerous jobs imaginable.

I wandered over to the green metal incinerators, lured in by the heat mirage they were creating. When I peered over the top, I could see bones scattered all over the bottom. Leg bones, arm bones, pelvises, skulls, big and small. The incinerator next door had just been fired up, and the wind was wafting ash all over us. We were wearing masks, and the burning had eradicated the virus, but it was best to leave.

As I walked away, I thought about how insignificant life seemed. People waste so much time worrying about trivial things, and we all end up as a bunch of bones in the ground, whether you're a king or a poor Liberian struck down by Ebola.

When we returned later, the incinerators were filled with white plastic body bags, which had been dropped off in our absence. The bags had jagged edges, where rigor mortis had set in, and leaked a lethal brown cocktail. A pickup arrived and the driver shouted at us to stop filming. The cameraman did as he was told, before the driver picked up a small body bag, carried it over to the incinerator and gently dropped it on top of the pile.

There was a name written on the bag: Morris. Was this the little boy we'd filmed at the UNICEF care centre? The bag was the right size. If this was the Morris we'd met, he was a happy little boy with a family only a few weeks earlier. Now he was being piled up like rubbish, about to be burned with a load of people he never knew.

Workers sprayed the incinerator with chlorine solution and closed the lid, squashing the bodies as they did so. They bolted the lid down and sprayed it again. Finally, they fired up the incinerator and the bodies started to burn.

CHAPTER 8

Tough Decisions: Find Your Passion

I arrived home from Africa three days before Christmas. I had to quarantine for 14 days, but it wasn't as if I had mates phoning me asking if I wanted to go for a pint. Hanging out with a bloke who had just returned from a two-month trip to an Ebola hotspot wasn't that appealing. Mercifully, after three or four days holed up in my bedroom, it was obvious I hadn't brought the virus home with me.

I'd seen terrible things as well as miraculous moments. But I didn't book up to see a counsellor, like I did after returning from Iraq. By then I'd worked out that the best form of counselling was to discuss what I'd seen and how I felt with anyone who wanted to listen. I talked it out, had become more pragmatic, was able to compartmentalise my experiences. But, like with Iraq, it cemented the urge to grab every single moment of life and make it worthwhile.

My wife and I spent a pleasant Christmas together, but I knew the marriage was doomed, only a couple of months after our wedding. I just wasn't sure it was possible to maintain a relationship while living a life of adventure. When you're working in TV, you have to take every job that's offered, because you might go for long periods without any work. And once I was on the job, I had to focus on what was necessary, and deal with any fallout on my return. There's that ability to compartmentalise again.

Looking back, I could have tackled the problem head-on when I returned from Africa and said, 'You know what, this isn't working. We want different things and it's cruel of me to keep dragging it out.' Instead, I took the cowardly route again.

In March 2015, less than three months after returning from Liberia, I flew out to Madagascar for two months to work on a History Channel documentary about pirate ships, on a paradise island called Île Sainte-Marie. I was working with a crack team of directors and producers who would later become good friends: Sam Brown, Joe Keenan and Tom Cross. Getting those diving qualifications had paid off almost immediately.

The shoot on Île Sainte-Marie overran though, so I desperately had to find someone to replace me. Luckily, I knew just the man. Jason Fox, presenter of Channel 4's *SAS: Who Dares Wins*, was one of my best mates from the Marines. When I went off and became a sniper, Foxy joined the Special Boat Service (SBS), but we'd always stayed in touch. Foxy was medically discharged from the SBS in 2012, after suffering with PTSD. He had problems adjusting to civilian life, as so many soldiers do, and at this point *SAS: Who Dares Wins* hadn't yet taken off. So when I asked if he fancied a month's diving off the coast of Madagascar, he almost bit my arm off.

Foxy and I were in Île Sainte-Marie together for two days, before I had to fly home. I was back in Bristol for no more than a couple of weeks before I flew out to Venezuela, where the TV adventurer Steve Backshall was doing some filming. Once again, that gig didn't happen by chance: one of the people who'd turned up to the pub gathering I'd engineered in Bristol had got in touch to say Steve was looking for a safety guy.

My destination was Canaima National Park, which is a UNESCO World Heritage Site about the size of Belgium – why is everything about the size of Belgium? – on the borders of Brazil and Guyana. Canaima is famous for its tepuis (meaning 'house of the gods'), which are table-top mountains of sandstone with almost vertical sides. They've been around for hundreds of millions of years, since before South America and Africa split. Canaima is also home to Angel Falls, named after Jimmie Angel, the US pilot who first flew over them. It is the highest waterfall in the world at 979 metres, which drops off the top of Auyán tepui and was only 'discovered' by Westerners in 1933.

Steve made his name as a TV naturalist (his wildlife knowledge is off the charts) but had by now carved out a niche as an explorer. His expeditions were about doing things nobody had done before, in this case exploring these mysterious tepuis. I was nominally there as head of safety, but was also the medic and organised most of the logistics. On top of that, I ended up appearing on camera. They were just little pieces, but there's an adage in TV that the next person to appear on the box is already on it, meaning they're part of the crew. And while I was quite happy doing what I was doing, occasionally showing my face couldn't do any harm.

Even today, Canaima National Park is not accessible by roads, so it feels almost untouched by humans. Canaima means 'spirit of evil' in the language of the local Pemon people. In fact, Canaima was the inspiration for Arthur Conan Doyle's book *The Lost World*. We spent three or four weeks exploring its hidden nooks, which felt like proper Indiana Jones stuff. It was everything I joined the Scouts for, everything I joined the Marines for: being outside for weeks, completely cut off from civilisation, living off my wits and my fieldcraft skills.

The tepuis' sheer-sided cliffs make them inaccessible to most humans – they're often described as islands in the sky – and they act as a refuge for rare plants and creatures. Their summit areas range from a few square kilometres to Auyán tepui's eye-watering 700 square kilometres.

We were climbing a tepui called Amaurai, the top of which no one had ever seen. The climb was to take seven days and proved to be a very spicy experience. It involved sleeping in hammocks or on rock ledges, dodging scorpions and getting caught in some horrendous weather. One day, we were enveloped by a massive, localised tropical storm. We knew we were in trouble when we saw the birds flying in to roost. In the middle of it, I had to abseil 200 metres to the ground to pick up a load of bags, change some batteries and what not. And as I was jumaring back up (jumars, or ascenders, are pairs of devices used for ascending ropes), things took a turn for the worse.

It was pitch black and I was hanging on the rope above the jungle about 150 metres up and three metres out from the wall. Venezuela competes with the Congo for the most lightning strikes per year, and soon there were flashes going off all around me. I couldn't look up because of the torrential rain and the water running off the top of the tepui in sheets. Rocks were tumbling down from above, and I could hear them crashing into the trees around me and exploding. It was hairy.

The wind was spinning me round and round and freezing me to the bone. I was stuck there nervously for about 40 minutes, until the storm passed as quickly as it had appeared. When I finally made it to our Portaledge, I was exhausted, drenched and shivering. But I spent the next 20 minutes looking out over the jungle, watching the lightning scuttling around and thinking, 'This is just so cool.'

Alas, we never did make it to the top. We hit a horrible section of rock and one of our team fell 15 metres and was very lucky to escape with a few scratches. After a pretty full-on team meeting about failed objectives, we all decided that to carry on in the face of that amount of danger was foolhardy. Nobody wanted to die out here and sometimes you have to know when to quit. And we learn our biggest lessons in the face of failure.

The park is home to five endangered animals – the jaguar, ocelot, giant anteater, giant armadillo and giant river otter – while 29 of the park's bird species and a third of its plant species are found nowhere else in the world. Although we weren't able to reach the summit of Amaurai tepui under our own steam, we made the decision that if we couldn't climb up then we *wouldn't* use the helicopter at our disposal to get there. Luckily, we were able to fly up to another tepui and what we found up there had been seen by very few sets of human eyes. There were towers of rock that resembled totem poles, deep gorges and tiny tepui frogs which lived in strange tubular plants like teacups, called pitcher plants. Everything was shrouded in strange mosses and lichen, and the bright emerald and ruby red hummingbirds were truly spectacular. There were even mammals up there, such as opossums.

Our Italian expedition leader, Francesco Sauro, from the Italian cave exploration and geographical organisation called La Venta, had been exploring for a few years before we turned up. Until recently, people didn't think there were caves inside tepuis because the quartzite sandstone was believed to be too hard. But the cave system inside Auyán tepui was vast, mile upon mile of passages and underground rivers, surrounded by giant boulders. There were lakes dyed metallic blue by bacteria and columns that wouldn't have looked out of place in a painting by Salvador

Dalí. The water had created a chemical reaction with the rock and rotted the caves from the inside (those interior collapses also caused the gorges on the summit), so those columns were literally propping up the ceiling. There was life down there, too. We saw giant aquatic crickets, probably endemic to that tepui. Steve even identified the bones of a big cat, probably an ocelot and thousands of years old.

After a few days of exploring, we decided to break new ground. We spent hours slithering through tiny gaps between collapsed rock, like giant earthworms, knowing that one misplaced hand or foot could bring hundreds of tons of tepui crashing down on top of us. We followed the river until we came to a waterfall, tumbling into the cave below. Above it was clear blue sky. Looking up, I thought to myself, 'This is what life is all about, seeing things that have never been seen before.'

Then we spent three days abseiling down Angel Falls, sleeping on ledges on the way. How many people can say they've done that? It was as scary as it was exhilarating. A totally addictive feeling.

For my next adventure I was embarking on a two-and-a-half-month drive from London to Asia. Yes, you read that correctly. *Helluva Tour* was a Channel 4 series involving four strangers travelling from the UK to Australia in a pimped-up Rascal camper van and getting into all sorts of scrapes along the way. I was wearing many hats as usual, including expedition leader, head of health and safety plus security/route consultant.

It was a cracking trip until, that is, I bowed out in Laos as planned, handed over the reins to someone else and my wife flew in to meet me for a holiday. For 10 days, we barely spoke. Even when we were in a hot air balloon together above the mighty Mekong River, which should have been magnificent, there was a defeated silence. By the time we got home to Bristol, the relationship was clearly over.

Sadly, my overriding emotion by that stage was relief. I had known it was coming. You only get one life, and I didn't want to spend mine in a relationship that wasn't making either of us happy. But by my actions, not hers. Being brave and making a necessary decision was something I was so good at in dangerous situations. Making tough calls about my life choices was more difficult.

Whether it's a job that pays well and affords you a big house, a flash car and a nice holiday once a year but that you don't enjoy, or a relationship that doesn't reflect your true self, if you're not happy or you're reining yourself in, you're not being the real you. You become a pale imitation of what you could be, what you should be, what you have a duty to yourself to be.

CHAPTER 9

50 Days, 10 Hours and 36 Minutes: The Power of Endurance

The divorce was finalised in no time. And how did I deal with it? By rowing across an ocean and processing my sense of regret – at the fact it didn't work out and that I was probably the cause.

As with many ridiculous challenges, this one started down the pub. One of my drinking buddies that night was Ross Johnson, a sniper partner of mine in the Marines and a sniper in his own right back in the day. After leaving the Marines, and a stint doing security in Iraq, he'd become a banker in the City. The other two madmen in the pub that night were also in banking: Matt Bennett, a former military policeman, and Olly Bailey, who had worked in various sectors, including advertising, film production and agri-tech.

The only things we all had in common were that we were pretty fit and pretty reckless. So over the course of a few too many beers, we came up with the idea of rowing across the Atlantic Ocean together, despite the fact that none of us had done any ocean rowing before. Before chucking out time, we even had a name: Team Essence. It sounds like a team name from *The Apprentice*, but essence is a term used in the Marines to describe something of beauty, such as an 'essence car'.

Matt did most of the planning, and before we knew it, he'd raised enough money to buy a 60-grand boat, which we called

Ellida, and had entered us into the Talisker Whisky Atlantic Challenge, which runs from La Gomera in the Canary Islands (off the north-east corner of Africa) to Antigua in the Caribbean. There was no going back now for the self-styled 'rogues of ocean rowing'.

Around this time, Ross and I went to put the world to rights over some beers with Foxy. He had already filmed the first series of *SAS: Who Dares Wins*, but it hadn't been broadcast and he didn't know how big it was going to be. While our Madagascan diving gig had opened up a whole new world to him, and I kept telling him that he could be doing exactly the same work as me, he was going through one or two personal problems and feeling a bit useless. That made no sense at all, given the skills Foxy had and what a great bloke he was. So we all asked him if he wanted to row the Atlantic with us.

At that point in his life, I think Foxy wanted to do something that would take up every second of his time and headspace. So he signed up almost immediately. I got the sense that we all wanted to row away from something, whether it was a bad relationship, a relationship that had just ended, a job that was causing unhappiness, or no work at all. And it seemed like the purest form of adventure: a journey with an unknown outcome. We had no idea what might happen or if we'd make it across. Maybe we'd all die and our boat would never be found. (Some of us might have been hoping for this: even container ships go missing at sea.)

By now, our PR and fundraising campaign was in full swing, but then we hit a snag. When Matt got in touch with the race organisers to tell them about our extra man, he was told that five-person teams weren't allowed. We'd bought a boat and already raised quite a lot of money for the NSPCC, but now had no race to row in. So we came up with an even bigger challenge: instead of rowing from La Gomera to Antigua, we were going to be the first team ever to row from mainland Europe to mainland South America.

We'd been through all the Guinness and Ocean Rowing Society records, and it appeared that no team had even tried it, so we might also set a new world record. What that record might be was a mystery. The Talisker record was 37 days, but by going from Portugal to Venezuela, we were adding an extra 900+ miles (the Talisker route is just under 3,000 miles). That meant we'd probably be at sea for a couple of months. The funny part was, I'd only recently flown that exact same route in the opposite direction, which took about 10 hours.

At this point you might be thinking, 'How the hell did Aldo find the time to train for a row across the Atlantic, what with all the other stuff he had going on?' The answer to that question is simply, I didn't. After agreeing to be part of Team Essence, I spent a month in Venezuela with Steve Backshall and two months driving from the UK to Laos. When 2016 rolled around – and with the embarkation date of 7 February looming large on the horizon – I was almost kicked off the team.

The other four rowed across the North Sea together, but the only training session I took part in was supposed to be an overnight row off the coast at Burnham-on-Crouch, on the Essex coast. Instead, we ended up rowing back to shore and hitting the local pubs. To be fair, I also attended a team bonding weekend at Glastonbury Festival.

I know Matt was pretty pissed off with me, but it wasn't really my fault. I didn't have a normal job where I could just take a weekend off to go rowing. And I didn't think rowing could be that hard anyway. As far as I was concerned, it didn't have much to do with technique and was more about being comfortable with discomfort, which I was pretty good at. So I kicked up a fuss and told them they couldn't kick a mate off the team. That did the trick.

People had told us that what we were attempting was foolhardy. Not only were we adding nearly 1,000 miles to the usual route, but we were also doing it entirely unsupported, unlike the crews in the Talisker race, who had safety boats and other teams around them. We also didn't have the same safety paraphernalia, like rafts and flotation devices – we needed that space for the food for the extra mouth we had to feed. The only person giving us any help was Foxy's dad, who was also a Royal Marine as well as being a keen sailor and a ninja weatherman. He'd be weather planning and navigating our course every day, telling us where the storms were and how to avoid them. But we were all fit, strong lads – three of us ex-Marines – so we had this supreme confidence. Of course we were going to do it. There was never any doubt. We felt like those ancient mariners, heading into the unknown on a voyage of discovery to conquer new lands and then burning their boats on the beaches.

Don't worry, we didn't actually burn our boat on the beach. But our final preparations were far from ideal. I only got back from a three-week job on Reventador volcano in Ecuador on Christmas Eve, and we were leaving for Lagos, our departure point in Portugal, in late January. Obviously, you can't put a boat on a plane, so we had to tow it from Matt's flat in Shoreditch, East London to Portsmouth, before sticking it on a ferry to Santander. We then had to drive all the way down to Lagos, where we had a week to dot the i's and cross the t's. Which, in reality, meant getting drunk and watching the weather.

I didn't feel much like an ancient mariner on the morning of our departure. We'd spent the previous evening out in Lagos and fallen into bed at about 3am, needing to be on the beach four hours later. It was like a comedy sketch. We'd already prepared the boat and taken it out for a few spins around the harbour, so it was just a case of loading up our washbags and waterproofs and personal comforts. But just as I was about to climb into the boat, I pressed the wrong button on my phone and deleted all my music. I had the hangover from hell, I'd never rowed before and now I was going to be at sea for maybe two months without any tunes. I did my best not to look furious, but I was raging inside.

On the plus side, the weather was perfect. As a crowd started to gather, including a few loved ones and local press, the adrenaline started pumping. On the minus side, just getting out of the harbour was hard work, despite all the cheering and waving. And then Ross suddenly announced he was feeling seasick. I smiled grimly and had to stop myself saying, 'Not a problem, Ross, you've only got 6179 kilometres to go ...'

Lagos got smaller and smaller, and soon it was just us and the sea. And when dark descended, it suddenly hit me just how monstrous this challenge was. Once Lagos had dipped over the horizon, our only light came from the navigation panel, and its compass pointing west. The adrenaline and my hangover had worn off and I felt drained and apprehensive. And my arse was already killing me.

To lift the spirits, as well as our temperatures, I decided to get a brew on. But when I asked where the tea and coffee were, I was met with deathly silence. After a couple of minutes rummaging through the bins, Ross finally admitted he'd forgotten to pack it. You could have cut the devastating silence with a knife. On reflection, whoever appointed Ross tea and coffee monitor needed their head testing, because he doesn't drink tea or coffee. Nevertheless, Ross had made a colossal blunder on day one, and we weren't going to let him forget it, even if he was spewing over the side. We'd spent a week cutting any packaging down to size, including tea bags and coffee sachets. And in the military, nothing raises flagging morale like a 'hot wet'. The thought of rowing all the way to Venezuela without a single cup of tea almost made me weep. For two months, all we had to drink was desalinated sea water and some spirits for celebrating milestones.

The boat, beautiful as it was, wasn't designed for five blokes. It was about seven metres long, and Foxy and I were in a cabin at one end, while Matt, Ross and Olly were in a cabin at the other. That might sound like there was plenty of room, but Foxy is a bit of a lump. We also shared our one-metre-tall and one-metre-wide cabin with our two bags, various instruments and rowing gear, which meant we just about had enough space to spoon each other. Not that I had a problem spooning Foxy, because it was bloody freezing.

There was space for two people to row at a time, which in theory meant that the other three would be resting. But we had a system of two hours on and two hours off, which didn't give us much time to do anything, let alone catch a few Zs. The chopping and changing of positions, including clipping and unclipping ourselves from the nylon line along each side of the boat (so that we wouldn't be swept away if we capsized) was quite fiddly and took a couple of weeks to master. By the time we'd crawled back into our cabins, dried off, had something to eat, done our admin and brushed our teeth, there was only about an hour and a half until the next shift.

I didn't sleep at all that first night. I remember looking up at the stars through the cabin's hatch, while waves came smashing down on top of us, and feeling very, very small and insignificant. Occasionally, I'd glance at the navigation screen in the cabin to see how far we had to go. The number didn't tick down very often.

It soon became clear that I'd be getting no more than a few hours' sleep in a 24-hour period, and only during the night (the maximum was four hours in a 24-hour period, split over two shifts). During the day, the light streaming through the hatch would be too bright. Personal admin became crucial. Sometimes after a shift, I'd be drenched and cold and feel far too tired to change my kit. But I had to, because otherwise my body would literally rot.

It was also someone's job every day to desalinate some sea water and make dinner. That involved filling up the Jetboil and hanging it on a hook to keep it upright. Then you'd cut the tops off five sachets of dehydrated meals and wait for the water to boil, before attempting to pour the scalding water into the bags while the boat was rolling from side to side. When the weather was bad, it was a hair-raising process – less a case of pouring the water into the bags than pouring it in their general direction. You'd stir the contents of the bags and let them stand for about 10 minutes before serving them up to often ungrateful crewmates. There were six or seven options, including chicken curry, vegetable lasagne, vegetable pasta, Thai rice and chilli con carne. But after a while, chilli con carne was all that was left, because everybody hated it.

Those first few days were about establishing some kind of rhythm, which is difficult when your oars are hardly ever in the water at the same time, you're getting smashed by swell and you're rowing backwards at a slow rate of knots. Once Lagos

125

had disappeared, we didn't see land again for seven weeks, besides the odd far-off dot. There was little boat traffic during the first week, and on the third night I'd just come on shift when I suddenly caught a waft of diesel. We had a powerful laser, which was actually illegal, so that if we saw a tanker, we planned to shine it through the bridge window to let them know we were there. I couldn't see or hear anything but after a very tense 20 minutes or so, this great big container ship loomed up beside us, no more than 100 metres away. Ross grabbed the laser and did what he had to do, but we had no idea if they saw us or not. Not that it made much difference by then. Once the wave created by the ship hit us, it was all we could do to stay upright.

That first section, heading down to the Canary Islands, was double grim. Minus tea or coffee, the only joy was provided by jelly babies and the occasional distant pod of dolphins or orcas. It certainly wasn't provided by the back-spray whenever some-one pissed off the side of the boat. On every expedition, there are things that no one mentions during the planning phase. And strangely, the subject of golden showers hadn't been raised down the pub.

Before a week was out, I'd lost so much weight from my arse that I could feel my bones grinding against the seat, which was just a standard seat you'd get on a rowing machine. I'd be stiff as a board before starting a shift, and then have to endure two hours of agony. We all ended up fashioning cushions out of foam and sheepskin. Sheepskin has lanolin in it, which is supposed to stop you getting infections, not that it seemed to make much difference. As the appointed medic, I was kept busy. Cuts and ingrowing hairs don't sound like much, but if ignored they can develop into something far nastier. Like that unfastened button in the military. Soon enough, Olly got an ingrowing hair on his foot that quickly developed into an abscess, almost down to his bone. Every day, I was cleaning it out with iodine and packing it.

Physically, I knew Foxy and Ross had what it took, because of their Commando experience. And despite being unknown quantities, Matt and Olly were lions on the oars.

On the mental front, it was all about focusing on process, process, process. Being ex-Marines, Foxy and I were used to 'keeping our shit in one sock', as the old military phrase has it, so our cabin was normally clean and tidy. We were also used to looking after each other. When Foxy came off shift, I'd have already made his bed (rolled out his damp sleeping bag onto the cold floor), laid out some dry kit for him to change into and put some toothpaste on his toothbrush. By looking after him, he'd be able to look after me, and everyone else. The other lads' cabin didn't run quite as smoothly, which must have driven Ross mad. Nevertheless, Matt and Olly displayed tremendous mental fortitude. They were able to stay in the moment, ignore the unnecessary and focus on the fundamentals of life: graft, food, water, personal admin and sleep, if possible.

It might sound strange, but the challenge was a form of therapy. I'd had to turn down work to do it, and didn't know when the next jobs would come in. I was still sorting out the practicalities of the divorce, like selling the house and settling bills. But in that boat, I forgot about all that. I was 100% in the moment, because I had to be. It was the same when I was a soldier in Northern Ireland, hiding in hedgerows all day gathering information, or a sniper, holed up in a hide for a week. Or when I was crawling through tight squeezes in a cave. It was just me and the environment, which made me feel every bit as insignificant as an insect crawling across my foot or a fish beneath the oars. Feeling insignificant usually has negative connotations, but it doesn't have to.

On that boat, one square metre was my life – the area I had to operate in, to have control over. Everything I needed to survive the next 10 minutes, the next hour, the next day and the next week was in that one square metre. The people with me in that one square metre were the only people in the whole world who mattered. It was mindfulness on steroids, living in the moment and reaching a place where nothing else beyond that square metre mattered. And when you've got five people in that square metre also in the same mental place, you can do the most amazing things together.

Pain is something else that's supposed to be bad, but there's nothing better to focus the mind. Every time I sat down for a shift and felt that terrible pain in my arse, nothing else mattered. Every time I gripped the oars and felt the terrible pain in my blistered and calloused hands, nothing else mattered. Every time I looked at the Raymarine nav system and worked out how long we still had left – thousands and thousands of miles – nothing else mattered. Everything apart from propelling that boat forward was just trappings, and trappings – physical and mental – overwhelm and sink so many people.

I don't expect rowing across the Atlantic to be everyone's cup of tea, but any form of graft that keeps you 100% in a state of flow, even in some pain, is good for you. I have always been attracted to that type of all-encompassing activity. When you are completely battered by the environment and immersed in the job in hand, there is rarely time for anything else. Our ancestors were doing a hard day's manual labour, before eating dinner, conking out and doing the same thing the next day and the next. If you spend all day sitting behind a desk, a run after work could make you too tired to worry about anything else before falling into bed. Or you could go for a long walk and connect with nature: feeling the change in temperature and the wind and rain on your face, noticing the leaves changing colour. When you immerse yourself in nature, many things seem clearer. I often go for a long hard run in the morning to use up excess energy and to think problems through; rarely after physically hard work or exercise do I have time or inclination for worrying or negativity. It sounds simple, because it is.

On the one hand, passing the Canary Islands was a big milestone: 'We've rowed all the way to where people go on their summer holidays!' It took us about three weeks, but we barely even saw land on the horizon. And it soon became clear why nobody had chosen our route before, and why none of the three or four crews who have tried our route since have made it much further than the Canaries. There are three converging ocean and weather systems in the region: the North Atlantic, the South Atlantic and the weather coming off the African mainland. That makes for stormy, choppy conditions that no rowing boat should be in. For a few days, we spent more time going backwards than forwards, which is hugely demoralising when you are giving everything that you have. You always keep on pushing as the tides and currents will change at some point. But then the conditions started to get really nasty.

The higher the waves got, the smaller I felt. And the harder the wind blew, the more inconsequential I felt. We couldn't get the boat to go in one direction, so eventually we pulled our oars in, put out our para-anchors (which are basically big parachutes that inflate under the water and slow down your drift, without completely stopping it), crawled into our cabins and battened down the hatches.

It's hard to describe how vulnerable we were, locked inside a boat the size of a sofa in the middle of a huge Atlantic storm. The swell was six metres high, so it was like being a cork in a washing machine. There was constant banging, as waves came crashing down on top of us, and every now and again a rogue wave would smash into us from the side. At one point, a huge wave hit us with a sharp profile and we were lifted up high and fast before the tether of the para-anchor snapped tight, almost stopping the boat dead in its tracks. Foxy was sent sprawling and went headfirst into the instrument panel in the cabin, smashing his face. Luckily, his teeth already looked like an SAS fighting patrol – excellently camouflaged and well spaced out.

The storm lasted about 20 hours, during which time we couldn't eat or drink. When it passed, I think all of us were probably thinking the same thing: the Canary Islands are only over there, we could just call it quits and row in. But nobody had the balls to say it. Instead, we cracked on. It helped that the wind and the sea were doing most of the work for us for once, rolling us in the right direction. We actually pulled the oars in, knowing the autohelm steering would keep us on course. For a while, things were exciting in a good rather than a frightening way. It was still a little scary, riding six-metre waves while clinging on to the sides of the boat, but then it got a lot, lot worse.

At 4am, in the middle of the ocean with a moonless sky, it is pitch black with only occasional glimmers of bioluminescence on the water or less occasional slaps in the face by stinking flying fish. Foxy and I were about to start our shift. I'd just swapped a sleeping bag with Matt and come up, as he and Ross were finishing their shift and Olly was heading inside. Then, from seemingly nowhere, a huge sidewinding wave smashed us beam-on and rolled underneath the boat, lifting us about nine metres up the face of the wave before slamming us down at what felt like 100 miles per hour. The boat capsized with monstrous force and I was thrown into the air until my tether snapped tight, before being slapped into water as black as tar and so cold it took my breath away.

There are few things more terrifying than being capsized at night in complete darkness in the middle of an ocean. But that's when my Marines training kicked in. Instead of panicking, I tried to come up with solutions. The first decision I made was simple: hold my breath for as long as possible or I'd drown. I could only hope that the others were also doing what they could to salvage the situation. I was under the water for what seemed an eternity – but I was at least attached to the boat, as were Matt and Ross. Inside the cabin, Foxy had been smashed around by the washing machine effect of the roll. After being submerged for about 40 seconds, I fought my way back to the surface, scrambled back onto the boat and started to climb up to the highest point to help Foxy weight it over.

Once we'd done that, it was about checking everyone was present and correct. That's when we realised that Olly hadn't been tethered to the boat when the wave struck (there were life jackets on the boat, but we hadn't been wearing them because they chafed while we were rowing).

Luckily, he'd fallen into the boat's gunwales and been able to cling onto the edge. Had he lost his grip, he would have died. No question. In fact, that same storm mowed into another rowing boat not too far away, tipping it over and sweeping a young lad off. And once you've been swept off in the middle of the Atlantic, there's no saving you. The hydrodynamics are so powerful, even an Olympic swimmer wouldn't be able get back to a capsized boat from a couple of metres away. Once overboard, you're just a piece of flotsam, at the mercy of the swell.

It was pitch dark, bloody Baltic cold, and everyone was in a state of shock. Water had got into the cabins and soaked our sleeping mats. And because they were made of felt and sponge, there was no chance of drying them out. Foxy had smashed his head – again. I'd lost my trainers and didn't have a spare pair, so I was going to have to row the rest of the way barefoot.

Foxy and I told the others to get back into their cabin while we carried out an inventory. We figured Olly needed a sit down, and the fewer people on deck the better. There was kit everywhere. We'd lost two of our three poo buckets (whenever we needed to empty our bowels, we'd have to whip out a bucket, plonk it down in front of whoever was rowing, pull down our shorts and sometimes even hang on to a rower's shoulders while we were evacuating). Thankfully, the navigation kit was all still present and working.

We'd worked out that the autohelm was trying to push us in one direction while the waves were going in another, which is what twisted the boat and rolled us over. But knowing that and being able to do anything about it were two different things. And then another gigantic wave fell on top of us. We both managed to stay on board, and the boat stayed upright, but water was pressurised into the hatch containing the life jackets, which suddenly inflated and blew open the hatch door, depositing the five fully blown life jackets onto the deck. Our only safety kit for the rest of the row was now compromised. The situation had descended into dark comic farce.

Foxy and I managed to gather up the life jackets and throw

them into the other lads' cabin, before deciding to put the para-anchors out. We were both showing signs of hypothermia – shivering uncontrollably, extremely irritable and not able to think straight – and the storm was still raging, so putting out para-anchors was easier said than done. Foxy kept shouting at me to throw them in and I kept telling him to stop shouting at me. Even in my befuddled state, I knew there were processes to go through. I managed to tie the necessary knots, despite my hands feeling like blocks of ice. But when I threw the second para-anchor out, it got snagged on the rudder. This was now a very dangerous situation. If the para-anchor ripped the rudder off, it was game over.

Foxy and I spent about five hours on deck, tidying up and trying to keep the boat going in the right direction as dawn broke. And we knew that as soon as the weather cleared, one of us would have to plunge into that inky sea and untangle the para-anchor from the rudder. Finally, the sun appeared over the horizon and the manes of the white horses became less wild. That was Foxy's cue to change into some shorts, put some goggles on, loop a rope around himself and jump in. That took a lot of balls. As well as being ridiculously cold, being attached to a rope in moving water isn't safe, because it's very easy to get pulled under the boat.

Mercifully, Foxy was able to release the para-anchor from the rudder, which wasn't damaged. But we still couldn't go anywhere. For the next 18 hours, we were bobbing around and trying to get warm, which was an impossibility. It wasn't until later that evening that the sea flattened out; we pulled out the oars and got rowing again. That was the only way we were going to warm up. And even if we ended up going backwards, at least we'd be busy.

Olly didn't have a military background and hadn't done a huge amount of outdoorsy stuff like the rest of us, so I worried about how he'd respond to almost dying. But he turned out to be incredibly resilient. Most people have that will to survive and recover quickly, it's just that they never know it because they spend their lives avoiding danger. Resilience comes from going through hardship. Now Olly knew what he was made of, the rest would seem easier. And there simply wasn't time to be reflecting on what might have been. As Foxy likes to say, 'Yes, you almost died. But you fucking didn't, so deal with it.'

There were five of us on that boat together, and we all needed to be strong for each other. Although Foxy wasn't quite as sanguine as he made out. When it had all calmed down, I overheard him screaming down the satellite phone to his dad: 'Why didn't you tell us about that fucking storm? It nearly killed us!' In fact, as Foxy would be the first to acknowledge, Silver Fox had actually done an amazing job keeping us safe and just to the fringes of the storm but we were wrung out and exhausted.

We didn't see Cape Verde as we passed it, but knew we were near land because of the changing smell and cloud formations. We were almost halfway through our row and still alive. All was reasonably calm for about a week, before we started motoring again. Having been rowing at three or four knots, the sea was now propelling us at 18 knots on big wave days. It felt like the boat was going to shake apart.

Foxy and I were in our cabin when we felt the boat listing once again, squashing us against the sharp corners of instruments. Through the hatch, we could see the other three, wide-eyed with fear, hurtling towards us as they desperately tried to push the boat over the back of the wave. And then we went right over again. We could see legs thrashing as they tried to scramble back on, and eventually they flipped the boat over.

It was daylight this time, so slightly less scary. But by now it was a war of attrition, an unending battle between us and the sea, with no truce in sight. Our sleeping mats were wringing wet again, as was almost everything else. Every time we cracked open the cabin door, we'd get hit by a wave. Both our para-anchors were damaged. Matt and Olly had lost their shoes in the second capsizing. Then, once we turned away from Cape Verde, the sea suddenly turned to treacle. It was calm and flat, but also thick and gloopy, so that it felt like we were treading water for long periods. One afternoon, a little brown bird landed on the back of the boat and stayed for two days. Like us, he was abso-lutely knackered. Unlike us, he could just chill out and recharge his batteries.

The pods of spinner dolphins, pirouetting with the grace of ballerinas before crashing back into the sea, were a rare joy. As were the fish with sails, that would ride the wind over the top of the water. But when we hit a section of fast-moving sea, we noticed we were being tailed by a massive shadow. That turned out to be an oceanic whitetip shark, which are famously aggres-sive and like eating shipwrecked sailors.

Not only had we almost been shipwrecked twice, but we desperately needed to scrape the algae and barnacles off the bottom of the boat because the drag was slowing us down. That wasn't a particularly attractive proposition at the best of times, but knowing there were killer sharks around made it even less so. When the shark finally disappeared after a couple of days, Foxy volunteered to do the first part of the clean. His climbing harness was attached to a rope, so that if the shark reappeared, I'd pull him in. Meanwhile, Ross had gaffer-taped a knife to the end of an oar, as a sort of makeshift bayonet. Had the shark reap-peared, it could have got very ugly, very quickly. I imagined

Ross being done for manslaughter, having accidentally stabbed Foxy to death.

We all had a crack at cleaning the underside of the boat, and it was a very surreal experience. You've got four or five kilometres of sea below you and you're scrubbing like mad with a wallpaper scraper, while looking over your shoulder and praying that the shark isn't going to make an appearance. Watching someone else do it was quite funny, because they'd look like they were on fast-forward. Doing it yourself was just a bit scary. While we were down there, we also took the opportunity to have a bit of a wash. That was a blessed relief, because by then we hadn't washed for about a month.

We also hadn't seen any signs of human life. Not only had we not seen the Canary Islands or Cape Verde, we also stopped seeing other boats (modern ships, being diesel powered, don't rely on trade winds and plough across in straight lines between Europe and North America). One day, we got a tweet from the astronaut Tim Peake. He wanted to let us know that despite the fact he was in the International Space Station, 402 kilometres above us, there was no person closer to us. That made me feel even more vulnerable: I was in a tiny boat in the middle of the Atlantic, and the closest human being was a spaceman!

When we reached the halfway point, in terms of distance, we cracked open some rum and whiskey, which had somehow survived the storms. There we were, the five rogues of ocean rowing, swigging whiskey and rum in the middle of the Atlantic. We'd battled through that messy convergence of weather systems, the weather was warming up and we now had a following sea, so getting all the way across suddenly seemed a distinct possibility. We'd got this far, so if we kept doing the same, we'd make it all the way. It's no different from walking. If you can walk across

France, there's nothing stopping you from walking all the way to China. You just have to keep putting one foot in front of the other.

Who knows what we'd have done if we'd had a support boat, like the guys doing the Talisker Challenge. There's a chance we'd have bailed out after the first capsizing, or maybe the second. But we didn't have a support boat, so we couldn't bail out. And turning around and rowing back was impossible. So we had no option but to suck it up and keep ploughing forwards. That's a good place to be psychologically. And it's a handy way to find a route forwards when you're at a loss. It might seem like you've got nothing left in the tank and that the only option is to quit. But the body will keep going until it literally falls apart; it's the niggling voices in your brain that will fool you into believing you're completely spent. Once you've travelled a certain distance, whatever the task might be, it makes no sense to chuck it all in. And chucking it all in will only make you feel worse, and so will looking back.

There were times during that row when we were all in awe of the sheer might and beauty of the ocean. But there were also times when we all hated each other and wanted to be anywhere else. I might not speak to someone for two days because they ate the chocolate pudding I wanted (we were burning 12,000 calories a day, so food issues could be quite upsetting), or I suspected they finished their shift five minutes early, or they left stuff lying around. I could be very short, snappy and a bit aggro. Other guys would fall into dark moods and not say anything for hours. But the bickering and the silences were symptoms of pain and discomfort and fear. And expeditions are all about dealing with those things – as well as the relentless monotony, countless irritations and borderline catastrophes – and just getting on with it.

137

Despite the little fallings-out over trivial things, everyone on that boat pulled their weight. And although it took a few weeks, we did eventually start working together as a proper team. It helped that we were all mates, although that doesn't have to be the case. As long as you're able to work with someone, you don't have to like them. On the flip side, you might have someone on an expedition who's great in 'real life', but a bad apple when the chips are down.

That old Commando pillar – cheerfulness in the face of adversity – was one of the most powerful tools. It never ceases to amaze me how dark humour can be. And the darker it is, the more useful it is. One day, Foxy had to take a bit of time off because of a swollen knee. When he reappeared that evening, he was carrying his trainers, which were clipped together with a karabiner. Foxy was very proud of his admin and the fact that he still had his footwear. He was making his way down the boat to his seat, clipped on to one of the tight nylon tapes running the length of each side of the boat. As the boat listed heavily, he pulled the tape back with all his force and let go of the trainers, catapulting them together at least six metres out into the oggin. It was one of the funniest things I'd ever seen. Foxy went apeshit, before jumping on the oars and rowing so hard that he broke one of the oarlocks and knackered his knee again. There were lots of sly looks and smiles, but no one had the balls to say anything. However, we absolutely annihilated him the following day.

A few days later, I noticed Foxy shifting around in his seat while he was rowing. We were all suffering, arse-wise, but he seemed to be particularly uncomfortable. Sure enough, as soon as our shift was over, he mumbled to me, 'Aldo, I need you to look at something.'

'What?'

'I'll show you ...'

Once we were safely ensconced in our cabin, Foxy dropped to his knees, pulled his kecks down and splayed his arse cheeks. I was on my knees behind him, with my arse hanging out of the door and my nose literally centimetres from his ringpiece. Thankfully, it was a calm day and the boat was quite steady, otherwise it could have got even uglier. As it was, next to his ringpiece was a disgusting green ingrowing abscess that looked like a creature from an early series of *Doctor Who*. I'd fought in a war, been inside a raging volcano and at the heart of a deadly pandemic, but nothing could have prepared me for getting up close and personal with the hideous thing nestled between Foxy's arse cheeks. I'm often asked if my life is glamorous. Well, this is your answer.

Every day for the next two weeks, I had to clean this wound out with iodine and repack it, just as I'd had to do with the abscess on Olly's foot. That meant putting my finger right in there, where no finger should be. Obviously, the other lads thought this was hilarious and were ripping us both to shreds. I remember saying, 'Can people please stop falling apart, because I'm the one who has to deal with all this shit. And we're so close to making it!' Then karma hit.

Over the next 48 hours, I came down with a terrible dose of galloping crotch-rot. Without going into too much detail, my undercarriage became covered in mould. It was very painful, but as far as the others were concerned, it was the most beautiful schadenfreude. As Mel Brooks once said, 'Tragedy is when I cut my finger. Comedy is when you fall into an open sewer and die.'

Because getting across the Atlantic required us to live constantly in the moment, we hadn't really thought about the practicalities of arriving. We hadn't told anyone where we were intending to land (we'd just said mainland South America), but our route was going to take us to a north-easterly point of Venezuela. We didn't have visas, and the waters between Trinidad and Venezuela – the Venezuelan mainland is only 16 kilometres from Trinidad – were some of the most dangerous on the planet, with fishermen, sailors and even tourists often hijacked and killed by Venezuelan drug traffickers and pirates.

So when the cloud systems started to change and we got to within a couple of hundred miles of Trinidad, we started to get worried. We were sitting ducks: five blokes in a rowing boat that couldn't go faster than four knots, and with no permission to be there. As we rowed in past Tobago, which was the first time we'd actually seen land since Portugal, we knew we had less than 36 hours left. The sun had just come up, the sea was flat and our spirits soared. At which point, a big motor cruiser appeared in the distance and started coming straight for us. For a few minutes, our hearts were in our mouths. Was it the police, coming to check our permits and turn us back? Or was it pirates, coming to kill us? Then we heard the cheering. It was Foxy's, Ross and Olly's partners, who had flown in from the UK and worked out where we were (with some help from Silver Fox).

We spent an hour or so shouting at each other from a distance – us looking like tramps, them lounging on the deck of their boat in bikinis – before we struck out for Venezuela. It was a memorable day to see land and people for the first time in seven weeks.

We rowed through the night, with Foxy navigating us in, before sighting land, switching off our lights and eventually sliding onto a gravel bank in near silence. It was pitch black and the beach couldn't have been more than 20 metres long, with jungle on either side. When we got off the boat, none of us could stand. Our legs, which we hadn't used in almost two months, were shaking and we kept falling over each other. It didn't help that I was off my tits on tramadol, because of the pain in my joints and two big abscesses in my legs. The karma had hit home hard by then.

We were obviously excited, but too knackered to even shake hands. To be honest, that landing was an anti-climax. We were also aware that we shouldn't be there, we had no paperwork or visas and were in potentially quite a dangerous spot.

We were so truly tired and broken by then. Even the smells were overwhelming. We hadn't been on land for so long and now we were assailed by the competing aromas of heat, sand, soil, rotting leaves and detritus. It all felt a bit *The Matrix*, in that I could almost see the odours.

After marking our position and making a little film, we knew we had to get out of Dodge. We pushed the boat back out, climbed back on and started rowing again – unfortunately against the current and wind this time. Four or five hours later, we were in international waters so could be picked up by the coastguard and towed back to a marina in Trinidad.

It was early when we arrived, standing on deck and soaking up the cheers. All the other lads were greeted by partners and family. I had nobody come to greet me, but I didn't feel left out. I'd rowed myself into an uber-happy place, so that I couldn't even feel the pain.

Standing on that boat, I thought, 'We've just rowed 6179 kilometres from Portugal to Venezuela in 50 days, 10 hours and 36 minutes, setting a new world record. More people have travelled into space or climbed Everest than have done that.' A crew might do it again. And they might beat our time. But they won't be able to say they were the first. That's what made it so special. It's easy to follow in other people's footsteps, because you know it's possible. It's far harder to do something that's never been done before. That takes a different level of character and tenacity.

CHAPTER 10

Cutting Loose: All Limits are Self-Imposed

I arrived home from the row at the start of April 2016 and I didn't have any work lined up until June. That was a difficult period. I wasn't depressed, but I did feel empty. And for the first time in a long time, I felt lost: 'What do I do now?'

In the space of just over a year, I'd travelled through the heart of a pandemic, dived for sunken treasure in Madagascar, explored tepuis in Venezuela, driven halfway across the world, rowed the Atlantic, and been married and divorced. Now I'd come crashing back to reality. I hadn't worked for months and while I'd just helped raise £250,000 for the NSPCC, I needed to pay my bills.

I'd moved out of our house in Bristol so my home, if you could call it that, was one of those showroom offices they have on new housing estates. Don't worry, I wasn't squatting, some kindly farmer had one on his land. I called it the 'Wendy house'. It had a sink and a bed, and that was about it. All my personal possessions were in one container and all my work kit was in another. I won't lie to you, there were times when I sat on my bed wondering where my life had gone wrong. I was 38 years old, single and living in a Portakabin. It was like a bleaker version of Alan Partridge and his static home. I didn't even have a friend I could visit in the BP garage.

TV is also a strange and precarious world. It can be fleeting as there's always someone else looking to take your job. I wondered,

'Nobody really knows what I'm supposed to be. Even me. Am I a rigger? Am I a safety guy? Maybe people think I want to be a presenter now and have left all that other stuff behind?'

Looking back, that post-row lull was essentially a spell of cold turkey. I'd become hopelessly addicted to adventure, and the thought of not doing something adventurous for a while was difficult to deal with. Now, I know how to deal with it. Whenever I arrive home from an expedition, I go straight into two or three days of decompression to stave off the emotional crash, including manic tidying and hoovering (I find hoovering incredibly relaxing!). Once that's out of the way, I start training again. But after the row, it took me a few weeks to shrug off the worry and the blues.

By June I was in West Papua (just west of Papua New Guinea), with Steve Backshall and a gang of Kiwis, who planned to be the first people to paddle the length of the mighty Baliem River (about 413 kilometres) – one of the wildest rivers in the world. I was head of safety on a white-water raft, bringing up the rear of the expedition. Steve had wanted me back, which was a boost to the ego. And, once again, I was attempting something that had never been done before. Just like that, all was right with the world again.

Before heading off down the river, we explored a huge cave system in the area that very few, if anyone, had ever explored before. About seven hours into this system, I was sitting precariously on a high boulder in the darkness, passing filming kit down to the film crew, when I slipped, fell about two-and-a-half metres and heard my ankle snap. Steve shot me a look that said, 'You better not be injured', and I told him everything was cool. But everything wasn't cool. We were deep into this cave system, with a three-week paddle down one of the nastiest rivers in the world to come, and I'd just nobbled myself.

After Steve had scrambled off ahead with the rest of the crew to do some filming, I went into shock. My vision changed from wide to pinhole dark and blurry and I was overcome by the most phenomenal pain. My stomach tied in knots and I started throwing up. Instead of taking my boot off, I tightened it up to stop the swelling and swallowed a load of heavy-duty painkillers. By the time the others got back, I was off my head on tramadol. But I was still trying to put on a brave face. It took about 12 hours to get out of the cave system, by which time my leg was black up to my knee. (A couple of months later, when I was giving a talk to some Manchester United players at their training ground – about resilience and fear, appropriately – one of the club physios scanned it and discovered that I'd snapped two of the three ligaments that join the ankle to the foot clean off.)

As it turned out, Steve and our team weren't able to paddle the entire length of the Baliem. We reached a particularly menacing section of rapids, which translated into 16 kilometres of certain death, so decided to call in our safety helicopter to drop us further downriver (a decision never taken lightly). We had to wait for three or four days because of the unseasonable weather, and when the helicopter did finally lift us out and drop us back further down, we were greeted by a bunch of very angry locals wielding spears and bows and arrows.

West Papua is the Indonesian half of the island of New Guinea. There's been an independence movement on the island since the Indonesians took over from the Dutch in 1962. Indigenous cultures have been sullied (some tribes have been completely wiped out) and their land destroyed by gold and copper mining, which hasn't made them any richer. All of which explains why the locals have a reputation for aggression – act now, ask questions later – and were so unhappy to see us.

Luckily, Steve spoke some Bahasa (the local language) – there's not much Steve can't do – and during a six-hour town hall meeting was able to convince the chiefs that we weren't there to take anything. After we'd all shaken hands and decided we were friends, I bought some of their beautifully crafted bows and arrows before bidding farewell. But I still didn't trust them. They knew where our camp was and could quite easily have ambushed and robbed us during the night. To be honest, I wouldn't have blamed them. I suggested to Steve that we quickly collapse camp and paddle a few miles downriver. That was quite a dangerous thing to do, because it was getting late and people are difficult to find if you capsize in the dark. But the alternative seemed riskier.

The deeper into the interior we travelled, the more alien the culture became. While that first gang of angry locals were clothed, in more remote settlements many of the men were naked apart from penis gourds. In some villages, some of the women were missing fingers. According to tribal tradition, when someone died, the oldest woman in the family had to have a finger chopped off, which was then buried with the deceased. The amputation, usually carried out with a stone tool, was said to ward off evil spirits and symbolise the pain of bereavement. These old women would be doing back-breaking manual work, gathering and cooking, with virtual stumps for hands.

That was a tough few weeks – I'm not sure I'd advise paddling down one of the most dangerous rivers in the world with snapped ankle ligaments – but I managed to hobble my way through and complete the expedition.

My brother Struan had kept the wind turbine business ticking over for a while but had now moved into TV, as a researcher on science programmes in Glasgow (he had studied molecular biology at university, rather than going into the military). So when Nick Jordan asked me to return to Mount Nyiragongo for a National Geographic series called *One Strange Rock*, I asked Struan if he wanted to help me with the safety. That was me saying thank you, for all those days he'd spent cleaning the inside of wind turbines when I was off abseiling down waterfalls or diving for treasure. I love that boy so much, but it wasn't all sentimental. I also knew he was a grafter, who I'd be able to rely on.

Nyiragongo had changed in the six years since we'd last been there. Conflict in the area had died down and Virunga National Park had become more tourist-friendly; there were even little huts at the top now. But there was still nothing friendly about the volcano itself. As we were arriving, a Belgian scientist called Benoît Smets, who had been studying Nyiragongo for years, was getting ready to leave. We shared a bottle of wine in his tent and he warned us that it was starting to become very active, although he didn't know why, which was disconcerting.

That first night, Struan and I sat on the edge as the sun was setting. I explained how Nyiragongo was different from before: the area around the lava lake had collapsed, so that the lake, now perfectly round, was further down. There was also a new vent on one side of the lava lake, basically a mini-volcano about 20 metres tall and making strange banging sounds, which was different to how this volcano normally behaves.

I looked at Struan's face, which was orange from the glow and stricken with fear. While I was soaking up the familiar sights, sounds and smells, and thinking how wonderful it was that my little brother was going to share the experience with me, Struan was thinking, 'I've got to actually go inside that thing ...' Just like me that first time.

Our job was to rig the ropes so that the crew could film an American volcanologist called Ken Sims, who is famous for collecting samples of rock in remote locations. Because I'd already been down there and remembered the way, I rigged the first part down to Tier 1 on my own. That was lonely work, with only a big bag of rope for company, banging in anchors for hours. Some of those anchors can fall out and rockfall could chop the ropes, so I rigged two sets, weaving my way down a 300-metre highly unstable ash slope, passing boulders the size of vans. Eventually, I made it down to Tier 1, where we'd used the Larkin Rescue Frame before.

Struan was a very experienced rigger, but everything is different in a volcano. Nothing is remotely solid and you need to be hyper-aware. Oh, and there's a giant lava lake below you. When he descended, he was wide-eyed. Not necessarily with fear, but with sheer awe. I was proud of Struan that day. Despite it being all new to him, he just got on with things and grafted. And him being there made it more of an adventure. It was certainly more exciting than cleaning out a wind turbine together.

This second time around, the plan was different. In 2010, we'd been going up and down, in and out of the volcano every day, which ate up a lot of hours and exposed everyone to unnecessary danger. This time, we set up camp on the largest 'ledge' inside the volcano – Tier 2, which ran most of the way around the inside of the volcano about 100 metres above the lava lake. That meant spending two or three days ferrying gear down: food, shelter, tents, filming and science kit – about 40 bags in all. Even water was needed for the entire team – one litre of water weighs a kilogram, and we had to take about 100 litres down. At one point, I even had a great big Honda generator strapped to my back. On top of that, until the camp was built we had to climb back up every evening to sleep in the new tourist huts. But it's my job to make things run more smoothly for the film crew. And the sight of the big green tepee – our 'mess' tent – surrounded by about 10 individual sleeping tents inside the volcano, all looking beautifully symmetrical, was a magical sight from the top.

While we were rigging, ferrying and building the camp, the film crew and scientists were still in nearby Goma. And the whole time, the vent – or mini-volcano – was getting bigger, louder and angrier. It was like a thundering cannon, regularly sending up mini eruptions of lava bombs that were landing on Tier 2, about 100 metres from our camp.

Once the camp was completed, I had to climb back up, race six or seven hours down the volcano to get back to Goma and collect the film crew and scientists. While I was away though, a freak thunderstorm blew in. Struan and the paramedic, Grant Thornes, were still inside the volcano while hailstones the size of golf balls clattered into their tents and created waterfalls all around the inside of the volcano. By the time I got back, the lads were quite shaken up. As was I, because the mini-volcano was now twice as high as when I had left.

Working inside a volcano is a constant war of attrition. We had to check all the ropes we had rigged (some of them had indeed been chopped by falling rocks) and our gear constantly. Tent poles and anything made of metal were already starting to corrode. The atmosphere even takes a toll on the body, with your fingers becoming pitted with glass, cuts becoming infected and your throat drying out because of the Pele's hair and poisonous gases. But we still had our job to do, which was to get Ken Sims and the film crew down to the bottom, erupting mini-volcano or not.

Before the final push, we were all mucking in with the science, collecting data and what not, which meant sleeping inside the volcano for about a week. I'd be lying in my sleeping bag, the tent shrouded in this intense orange glow. And all I could hear was the volcano's hydraulics, as if I was in some factory in hell. Sometimes, I'd wake up needing to put my gas mask on because the gasses were so thick. I'm not sure if it's the strangest place I've slept – there's a lot of competition – but it's right up there. And it was particularly terrifying because it sounded like the new mini-volcano was about ready to blow its top.

By the time of the final descent, as we began to accompany Ken to get the fresh lava samples he needed, lava bombs were landing all around us. At this point, Ken started having second thoughts. And this is a guy who had been in some of the most dangerous volcanoes on the planet. Nick and I were leading, had already completed the 10-metre abseil directly below Tier 2 and were descending the hazardous boulder field slope beyond that. I was about to start the final 80-metre drop when Struan, who was looking down on me through binoculars from the other side of Tier 2, got on the radio and said, 'Bro, don't go over the edge.' At this point, Ken had already started climbing back up to Tier 2.

I was the head of safety, but Nick's job was to get the most dramatic shots possible, so there was a conflict. To be honest: if we were both wondering if it was a good idea or not, that meant it definitely wasn't. Meanwhile, Struan and my old cameraman mate Johnny Rogers had grown even more anxious. And poor old Ken was even swearing, shouting at us to 'fucking stop and get the hell out of there', which is not the sort of thing eminent old American scientists normally say.

I told Struan not to worry, that I'd be down and up again in 10 minutes, before he informed me that the bottom of the cone-shaped vent, about 100 metres away from me and now grown to about 60 metres high, had started bulging. Then he started pleading. That was very strange to hear, because Struan's not normally like that.

Finally, he said, 'Maybe just see what it's like tomorrow.' Almost exactly as he said those words, I turned around while precariously perched on the crumbling edge and saw the bottom of the mini-volcano burst open. Within seconds, hundreds of tonnes of scarlet red lava were flowing as fast as water, lapping against the rock right below me; it truly looked like Mordor down there. The entire base of the volcano was raging with fresh lava and the thermal action whipped up hurricane-force winds. It was both spectacular and terrifying at the same time. We were inside a volcano while it was erupting. That was my cue to get the hell out of there, just as Struan and Ken had been telling me to do. Between them, they had saved my life. Had I ignored their pleas and abseiled down further, it would have been the last thing that I would have done on this planet.

Ken left the volcano that night, while the filming team stayed down there and drank whiskey in the mess tent. As you do when you've had a shave as close as that. There was another evening of collecting samples and filming, including some incredible sequences, before we said farewell to the film crew. Then Struan, Grant and I spent the next two or three days stripping the kit and bringing it all back up to the top. In the end, there was just one tent left inside, so Struan and I decided to spend one final night in the gateway to hell.

We were pretty wired, lying in that tent. The mini-volcano was still banging away and the bottom of the entire crater was covered in the fresh lava flow while the thermals, which were dragging cold air in from the top, created hurricane-force winds which were smashing up our tent. At one point the tent material was smothering our faces, and then the tent poles snapped. We might have asked each other, 'What the hell are we doing?' But I was so chuffed to have gone through that experience with my brother. Struan had conquered his fear and grafted his nuts off. A few years later, he'd be producing and directing documentaries of his own, and hiring me to work for him.

One of the great things about experiencing hardship is the feeling of getting back to civilisation after it's all done and dusted. When you've been living inside an erupting volcano for three weeks, you're absolutely knackered and you look like you've just returned from a war, then getting back to your hotel room, showering, falling into bed and pulling those clean, crisp sheets over you has to be one of the most beautiful feelings in the world. And when I got back to the UK this time, there was someone waiting to hear all about what I'd done.

I'd met Anna at the end of 2015. In the time between my divorce and rowing the Atlantic, I was doing a job on Reventador volcano in Ecuador, for a Discovery Channel documentary that Anna was producing. We kept in touch during the row and got together after I got back.

Now when I returned from a job, I was kicking the door down, because I couldn't wait to tell her what I'd been up to. Anna was a kindred spirit, an adventurer like me. And when another job came in, I didn't feel guilty, just as Anna didn't feel guilty when she had to disappear for a month, working on a documentary on the other side of the world. When we came home from doing our own things, we'd fold our experiences back into the relationship, making it stronger.

All the same, to some my life sounds like a chaotic nightmare. Even before I got home from the Congo, I was mentally packing my bags for China, where I was about to work on a documentary with Guy Martin, the mechanic and motorcycle racer who was forging a career as a TV personality. Straight after that, I would head to a diving shoot in Iceland for a clothing brand, before returning to Angel Falls for another episode of *Welcome to Earth*. After that, I was straight off to South Africa for an anti-poaching documentary, then on to the Maldives for another diving shoot.

The logistics – where and when, planes, trains and taxis – were mind-blowing. Plus, all those jobs required different kit, so I was constantly planning and packing in my head.

At this time, I had my van parked almost permanently at Heathrow. The most ridiculous sequence was Iceland–Venezuela–South Africa: I literally got off the plane from Iceland, dumped my diving kit in the back, checked in 20 bags of climbing kit, flew off to Venezuela, flew back to Heathrow, dumped my climbing kit in the back, checked in again, and flew to South Africa. My actual home was still a Portakabin on a farm but my days of feeling like a bleaker version of Alan Partridge were over. That Portakabin had everything I needed. And I was working and earning money. People think there's only the 9–5 way of living, but it doesn't have to be that way.

There were also family and friends to see – Mum, Dad, siblings, old military pals – visits and nights out. I need the pilgrimage to Scotland at least twice a year to recharge my batteries – not only are my family there but it's in my blood and the mountains are my home. Plus I had to fit in training and quality hoovering time.

Trying to sustain a personal life with all that going on is extremely difficult and you lose a lot of friends along the way.

Even when you do catch up with people, you don't want to be that pub bore who's constantly banging on about his latest exploits. So you don't tell them what it's like to abseil down Angel Falls, or be inside an erupting volcano, or almost drown in the middle of the Atlantic. Instead, you play everything down: 'Yeah, it was a good trip. Same old, same old . . .'

Don't get me wrong, I get it. Not everyone wants to hear about my adventures, they just want to have a chat about the football or what's on the telly instead. But my close mates from school and the Marines understand when they don't hear from me for months at a time. And it's why most of my mates now also work in TV, and why I ended up going out with Anna, because they *get* it. People who don't get it, who need a continuous dialogue and get upset if you don't reply to a text or missed call immediately, fall by the wayside. My personal life has become streamlined, so that I now have a set of what you might call 'thick and thin friends', people I can meet having not seen them for months or years and immediately pick things up from where I left off, without any awkwardness. They're true friends, because they're 100% on board with my life choices.

The best thing about working with Guy Martin is that he doesn't give a shit about television. He hadn't even seen any of his own programmes until the coronavirus lockdown, when they filmed him watching some highlights. With his persona, which is exactly the same on TV as it is in real life, Guy could be on all sorts of programmes. But he'd rather be at home in Lincolnshire, doing MOTs on lorries or sitting on his tractor, listening to podcasts and sowing potato seeds. He always has a job on.

At the same time, he's hugely astute and aware of his own value. He's also a proper grafter and up for pretty much anything.

In China, he set a world record for cycling the world's longest desert highway, 547 kilometres across the Taklamakan Desert, AKA the 'Desert of Death', in 28 hours and 17 minutes. (It was the third time I had been to the Taklamakan Desert – the first time was with Henry Cavill on *Driven to Extremes* and the second time was on that long overland drive to Laos.)

It was a producer called James Woodroffe who decided that Guy would work well on TV and I might work well with him – they are a tight-knit team that has worked together for years. (James directed the celebrity *Driven to Extremes* driving programme back in 2012 and would be master of ceremonies at mine and Anna's wedding.) James realised that he could make a virtue of Guy's eccentricity and lack of interest in being a TV personality. Just watching him drinking tea on a plantation, sitting cross-legged and struggling to get his fat farmer's fingers through the handle of a tiny bone china cup was funny. They wanted to film a shot of Guy watching the largest dam in the world – the giant Three Gorges Dam – it was the sort of production where you're there to film the opening of the dam, or something equally as spectacular, and you end up filming Guy under a forklift truck talking about bearings and nuts.

By 2016, I felt I knew enough about how TV worked – and what mistakes not to make – to start pitching ideas for programmes to work on and even making my own. There were literally hundreds of channels and organisations all over the world that needed content, and because my face was starting to appear on TV from time to time, commissioners were beginning to know who I was. The more I got involved with TV production, the more I wished I had found it sooner. But in life, we rarely get what we are not yet ready to receive.

I was determined to make a film about wildlife crime but my first pitch to be commissioned by the BBC was about Mount Nyiragongo – my nemesis. *Expedition Volcano* was filmed in June 2017 and broadcast in two parts later that year. On the recce, I got to hang out with mountain gorillas for the first time, which was an incredible experience and made me even more determined to raise awareness of wildlife crime. They are such beautiful creatures but super intimidating. One of them pulled a branch down on my head as a show of force, and I had to stand with my head bowed and arms tucked in, to demonstrate my subservience. He was a great slab of muscle and could have wiped me out with a single swipe of his arm.

Gorillas are perfect metaphors for the Congo, beautiful but dangerous. The Congo is one of my favourite places on earth, full of UNESCO World Heritage Sites, breathtaking scenery and endemic wildlife, such as the okapi, a strange half-zebra, half-giraffe creature that lives in the jungle. Even the country's huge abundance of natural resources has dark consequences. The coltan in your mobile phones and laptops is mined by children, and coltan mining has destroyed the environment and financed wars. In April 2020, four civilians and 12 Virunga National Park rangers, including some I had worked with, were massacred by Hutu militiamen. More have been killed since, which is why Virunga National Park is one of the most dangerous conservation projects in the world.

Before going inside Nyiragongo for a third time, we filmed a segment on the carbon dioxide produced by the nearby Lake Kivu. Carbon dioxide is heavier than air, which means it hugs the ground like a fog. Unfortunately, you can't see or smell it. In the Congo, the locals call it a 'mazuku', which means 'evil wind'. If you breathe it in, it sinks to the bottom of your lungs and can asphyxiate you.

One place we know should be avoided are carbon dioxide sinkholes, so we filmed a goat being walked into one to show the locals just how dangerous those things are. This goat promptly stopped breathing, before a scientist brought it back to life by giving it mouth to mouth. The scientist emphasised his point by staying inside a sinkhole too long and almost fainting. I had to jump in and pull him out, while holding my breath.

I was co-presenting with the TV doctor Xand van Tulleken and the geologist Chris Jackson, and we were working with the volcanologist Benoît Smets, who'd warned me the volcano was acting strangely the year before. He got that right.

This time, there were four of us rigging – me, Struan, Grant Thornes and my old Marines mate, Daz. I knew Nyiragongo well by now so things went smoothly, though the route down inside always changes due to rockfall and tectonics. Once again, we set up camp on Tier 2, and the mini-volcano had gone back to dozing, so we weren't afraid of being skulled by a flying lava bomb. My plan was to get all the way down to the bottom and the lava lake, before coming back up and bringing the camera crew and scientists, including Benoît, back down with me this time.

I descended slowly, hanging from a boulder the size of a house, which was in turn sitting right on the edge of an overhang. I had an almost overwhelming fear of the boulder coming loose and splattering me, or being asphyxiated by carbon dioxide. It was complete sensory overload blended with borderline panic. I knew how epic it looked and had asked several times for it to be filmed but all the camera teams were busy and the director assumed, wrongly, that we would get a second chance at it when we all went down. In my experience of adventure TV, there's rarely a second chance. I descended alone into the lowest and most dangerous part of the volcano while the crew filmed GVs (general views) up on Tier 2.

I was only the third person to make it to the lava lake level of Mount Nyiragongo, to stand on the solidified lava floor, but none of it was filmed – which I have to say was pretty annoying.

After gingerly jumaring back up, being careful not to use my feet because one false step might cause a rockslide of an unimaginable scale, I knew it was just too dangerous for anyone else to go down there. When Benoît saw me, he said, 'I can see just by the look on your face that it's a bad idea.' I must have looked haunted. Scientists tend to be rational people, documentary makers less so. But after a quick chat we all agreed to pull the ropes up and get out of there. The only footage of my descent was shot on my phone, which proved the TV adage: 'The best camera is the one you have in your hand at the time.'

Just a week later, Benoît sent me some drone footage taken from the top of the volcano. The stream of solidified lava I'd stood on was now buried in huge rocks. The whole boulder slope I'd abseiled down below Tier 2 had collapsed – hundreds of metres and thousands of tonnes of rockfall. Who knows when that had happened, but it could quite easily have happened when I was in there. Being an adventurer involves a lot of calculated risk-taking. But it also involves trusting your instincts and realising that sometimes you need to run away to live another day.

The slump was behind me, I was back to feeling amazing again, upright and pointing in the right direction. I had the 'adventure twinge' back, as I called it. Having seemed for a short while a precarious way to make a living, once again this was the only job in the world that made sense. Rowing the Atlantic had been a complete severing from the past, a cutting loose from my marriage and my previous business. Now I knew the life I wanted, and I could concentrate on feeding the real me.

Too many people avoid making big decisions. Everyone is a representation of the tough decisions they've made. Or haven't. To use a nautical analogy, making a big decision is like putting the rudder down and raising the sails, regardless of which way the wind is blowing. Most people leave their rudders up and their sails down, because going against the wind is hard work. Going against the wind also takes courage, to do what you know deep down is the right thing for you, even when most people are going in the opposite direction. Without hard work and courage, you might end up on the rocks.

CHAPTER 11

Narcos: Make the Decision

I know some people will think phrases like 'you become what you think about' are nothing more than words. But I was living proof that you can do whatever you want to do. I was exactly where I wanted to be. Anna would say, 'If £1 million suddenly appeared in your bank account, would you quit your job/ change your life?' And my answer, without hesitation, would be, 'No!'

I might wear more expensive clothes and have a more expensive car, but they wouldn't make me any happier. Clothes are just clothes and cars are just cars, however expensive they are. No one has ever been on their death bed and thought, 'I didn't do much. But at least I owned some lovely trainers.' But people will reflect on the amazing adventures they had. Or regret that they didn't have more.

I was doing exactly what I wanted to be doing, getting out there every day and tearing into life. And I'd proved another adage to be true, namely that if you find your passion in life, it no longer feels like work. My life was like being in the Scouts, but on a far grander scale and I was getting paid for it. And I was making decent money. Not millions of pounds, by any stretch, but more than I got for cleaning out wind turbines. If you have a passion in life – a real passion – it will pay. You might not become a millionaire, but you'll have enough money to be happy. I even managed to get decent time off, which is ultimately more valuable than money.

A couple of months before that third descent into Mount Nyiragongo, I moved in with Anna. When you follow a passion in life, you will meet someone as enthusiastic about it as you. Unfortunately, I was on a dive shoot in the Maldives at the time. Actually, scratch that: that gig was excellent. I was there for three weeks, living on a boat on the crystal-clear waters of the Arabian Sea for a National Geographic *One Strange Rock* shoot filming parrot fish. I'd wake up, eat some tropical fruit for breakfast and dive for a couple of hours, watching beautiful parrot fish munching away at coral with their beaks. Then I'd hop back on board for lunch, dive for another couple of hours, wrap up for the day, swing by a honeymoon bar for a couple of beers, before doing the same the next day.

Poor old Foxy had the job of moving all my gear (I'd call it 'gear', Foxy would call it 'tat') into the new flat in Tooting. I'm bound to say that's what friends are for, but Foxy didn't see it that way. I was drinking a nice cold lager while he spent the days lugging around heavy boxes. But this was a man who had knelt before me on a boat in the middle of the Atlantic, splayed his arse cheeks and asked me to take a closer look. He owed me.

In addition, I was about to follow Foxy on maybe the most dangerous mission I'd ever been on. And the most foolhardy. Foxy had become a TV personality by now through his appearances on *SAS: Who Dares Wins*, and he was branching out into documentaries. When Channel 4 commissioned him to make a three-part mini-series about South American narcos, he asked if I fancied joining him as head of safety and security.

I did have second thoughts. I'd only just got out of the volcano, so mentally I was fried. And this was something completely different. In the Congo, I was in charge of the rigging and dealing with natural hazards – poisonous gases, rockfalls, flying lava bombs – and the threat of armed militia. But Foxy's gig involved dealing directly with drug traffickers and hitmen (sicarios). As such, it seemed entirely possible that we'd be murdered. But it also seemed bloody exciting, so I decided to do it anyway. Sometimes, my decision-making is that simple.

Before leaving for Peru and the first leg of the shoot, I arranged with a company to track our vehicles and phones wherever we went. I also made sure we had as many contacts on the ground as possible, in case anything went wrong. Foxy was well-connected obviously and another company Secret Compass, an adventure travel company that also provides safety for the film and TV industries, did all the due diligence prior to the trip and kept us safe on the day-to-day missions from back in the UK. We'd be spending time in some very nasty places, like in the backs of strangers' cars with bags over our heads, so it was about making sure people knew where we were at all times. Foxy and I also had a conversation about the level of risk we were comfortable with. Were we comfortable being hooded in the back of a vehicle for 10 minutes? Yes. Were we comfortable being hooded in the back of a vehicle for half an hour? No. We had to know the answers beforehand, because we were on our own.

We started in Peru because that's where so much of the cocaine is produced. I already knew, from personal experience, how dicey the region could be. In 2004, I was doing some travelling around South America when the little internal plane I was on got busted for drugs. Then I got a bus down to the Peruvian city of Arequipa, which was hijacked. I was sitting right at the front, having a little snooze, when a brick came flying through the window. The hijackers pulled everyone off, took our money and held us there for seven or eight hours. No one was harmed, and I think they were political bandits rather than anything to do with drugs, but it was still disconcerting.

Shortly after landing in Lima, we met a guy whose job was to go to nightclubs, chat up girls, give them a couple of grams of coke and get them hooked, so that they'd eventually start working as mules. We watched him at work in Lima, slithering around this nightclub like a snake. These girls would end up smuggling 100 or 200 grams in their vaginas, and this horrible, predatory man would grass one out of every 10 to the cops. The poor girl would get maybe 10 years for trafficking and the guy would walk away with money in his back pocket.

You might be wondering why anyone would want to tell us this stuff. Everyone we spoke to on that trip, from low-level dealers to former associates of Pablo Escobar, had a gigantic ego. They loved the fact that films were being made about them, it made them feel important and their seedy lives vaguely glamorous.

Coca farmers aren't to blame for the cocaine industry. They're not drug dealers, they're just trying to get by within the social and economic framework of their country. People have been growing coca leaves in South America for thousands of years, and its uses are myriad. As a stimulant, it's long been used to overcome fatigue, hunger and thirst; as well as aches, pains and altitude sickness (I used to chew coca leaves in the high Andes when I was on climbing trips in my early twenties). It's also an important part of religious ceremonies. Only relatively recently did it start being turned into a white powder that people killed for.

A lot of coca farmers would rather grow something else instead, because of all the violence and destruction associated with it. But the reality is that they can grow three coca crops a year, rather than just one crop of avocados. Meanwhile, the government knows that if it torches the existing coca fields, they'll just pop up elsewhere. The government even buys a certain amount of leaves from the farmers, but they have to be perfect, whereas the narcos will take the whole lot and pay the same day, at three times the government's rate.

For the past decade, Peru has been vying with Colombia as the biggest cocaine producer in the world (Colombian production dropped off in the early twenty-first century because of a successful counter-narcotics policy, but it has rocketed again in recent years). The Valley of the Three Rivers (also known as 'Cocaine Valley' or the VRAEM Valley) consists of thousands of acres of coca fields, all of it grown legally. But even when they're selling their leaves to the narcos, the farmers make a pittance. Only when the coca leaves have been turned into cocaine does the real money kick in.

We filmed people extracting cocaine paste from coca leaves in what are called maceration pits (and a police raid to blow some pits up, although the producers were long gone). That paste then goes through various other chemical processes to turn it into the white powder people love to shove up their noses. From factories in the Peruvian jungle, the cocaine is smuggled to the capital Lima, before being distributed across the rest of South America.

If you wanted to buy a kilogram of pure cocaine in Peru, it would cost you about $2,000. The big boy traffickers are those who get it across the Mexican border and into the United States. In New York, a kilogram of cocaine might cost $30,000. That actually translates into even more money, because it gets 'cut' with so many substances along the way. So on the streets of New

York, someone might pay 25 times as much as a native of Lima, for a gram of cocaine that's far less pure.

Hanging out with coca farmers in Peru was reasonably safe, but things got a lot spicier when we moved on to Colombia. The first guy we hooked up with was Jhon Jairo Velásquez, otherwise known as 'Popeye'. (I don't know why Popeye was called Popeye, but it wasn't because of his love of spinach.) Popeye was a hitman for Pablo Escobar, who was head of the murderous Medellín Cartel until his death in 1993. He killed hundreds, if not thousands, of people, at Escobar's bidding. No one was safe from Popeye, whether you were a member of a rival cartel, a cop, a judge, a politician or an innocent bystander. In 1989 alone, Popeye masterminded the murder of a presidential hopeful and the bombing of a plane, which killed 110 people. Popeye was given a 30-year prison sentence in 1992 but released in 2014.

A fixer arranged for us to meet Popeye for lunch in Medellín, and when he walked into the steakhouse, people greeted him as if he was Jesus. They were bowing down and shaking his hand, and he was touching them on the head. When we sat down, the first thing he said to us was, 'If you'd walked in here on your own, you would have been killed.' He seamlessly moved on to boasting about all the people he'd murdered, without showing as much as a flicker of emotion, before asking if we'd ever killed a wife. When we answered no, the dead-eyed Popeye nonchalantly replied, 'I have.' He seemed super proud of it, as if he was telling us about a decent round of golf he'd played or a big fish he'd caught.

Popeye wasn't the sort of bloke I'd choose to spend time with, but he knew a lot of people and opened a lot of doors that otherwise would have remained closed. He was a celebrity in certain Medellín circles and even had his own YouTube channel. When we later went for a walk in one barrio (district) of Medellín, we stopped at a shrine to a child who had been shot dead in the street a few days earlier. Popeye had a quick and cordial chat with the family, before taking us to Escobar's grave in a peaceful cemetery just outside the city. The grave has become a macabre tourist attraction and kids sneak in at night to snort cocaine off the headstone. Popeye didn't snort any cocaine, but he did say a prayer to his former boss.

Afterwards, we went back to Popeye's home, which was a two-bedroom apartment in a non-descript high-rise. That was a weird, tense couple of hours. The walls were covered with narco artwork and paraphernalia, and Popeye was very keen to show us his collection of handguns. Popeye knew Foxy was a former soldier and seemed to think that made them kindred spirits. When the camera was rolling, he said to Foxy, 'I'm a murderer and you're a murderer. It's just that your murders were sanctioned by the government.' We could have spent all day philosophising about that, but it was better just to nod our heads.

When Popeye found out I was a sniper, he started interrogating me: 'What distance can you shoot someone from? Would it be easy to train civilians?' This was seriously surreal: the chief hitman for one of history's most murderous drug lords was asking me for tips on how to kill people. When he found out we'd rowed the Atlantic, you could see his mind whirring. Even I was thinking, 'I wonder how much cocaine we could have stashed in our boat?'

After the interview, which was a matter-of-fact rundown of Popeye's various killings, he insisted we pose for pictures with him. In one, he had a pistol to my head. I was looking at Foxy, thinking, 'This is insane. This guy has killed more people than he even knows.' Afterwards, he said to me, 'You're lucky. Most people who have my gun to their head don't live to tell the tale.'

Popeye then unfurled a wanted poster, with his and Escobar's faces on it, before pulling out a magic marker and writing on it: 'To my warrior friend Aldo. From Popeye, assassin for Pablo Escobar.' It now has pride of place above our living room mantelpiece. Ha. Not really. But I do still have it somewhere, as a reminder of two of the strangest hours I've ever spent. Not long after that interview, Popeye got banged up again for various crimes, before dying of cancer in 2020. I didn't shed any tears, but I'm sure some did.

Our next port of call was Buenaventura, a gritty port city on the north coast of Colombia. Buenaventura is a bustling hive of crime, full of guerrillas, paramilitary groups and drug traffickers. Unsurprisingly, the violence is off the scale. A few days in, I was getting some air on the roof of our dodgy hotel when I heard gunshots below. I later learned that someone had been shot in the café we'd had breakfast in. Foxy and the director were out doing a recce, and I had to tell them not to come back yet because the police had arrived and the streets were still buzzing. That was a wake-up call, because we'd been walking down that street every day, to get to a makeshift jungle gym on the beach.

The plan was to link up with some traffickers and witness the arrival and departure of a 1,000-kilogram consignment of cocaine (so a street value of $2,000,000 in South America and possibly $50,000,000 in the US). The drop-off point was a barrio right on the sea, all buildings up on stilts and built mainly of wooden planks. While we were waiting for the boat to arrive, the rest were inside one of the huts filming an interview with the bloke whose job was to paddle the consignment out to a big tanker. The consignment would then be taken out into the Pacific and dropped off wherever.

I was sitting outside this building in the dark while Foxy was inside with the cameraman filming when two blokes started walking down the street towards me. One had his hand behind his back. People assume I'm armed on these jobs, but that isn't the case. I wasn't armed in the Congo, Liberia or Sierra Leone, and I wasn't armed in Colombia. If people know you're armed, it immediately escalates the situation. It only makes sense to be armed if you've got hundreds of armed mates to back you up, like in the military. That's why I've had to develop other, softer skills, like empathy, learning to read delicate situations and talking my way out of problems.

When dealing with traffickers and sicarios, it was all about letting them be the alpha males. They knew we weren't weak, because we'd been Marines. But they made it quite clear that we were only alive because they'd allowed us to be. All the same, however magnanimous they wanted us to think they were, we couldn't trust them. They were hardened criminals and would have killed us at the drop of a hat, which was why we had to scarper when necessary.

On this occasion, I hissed through the door, 'Foxy, we need to get out of here.' The two blokes were now standing under a streetlight about six metres away. The one with his hand behind his back pulled it out, made it into the shape of a gun, pointed it at me and pretended to pull the trigger, before turning around and walking off. The director wanted to stick around to see the cocaine being delivered. This was supposed to be the crescendo of the film but Foxy and I overruled him. We switched the camera off and bailed in a hurry as the atmosphere had totally changed. Then, and just as we were leaving, we saw big slabs of cocaine being unloaded. No wonder they didn't want us around. Just because a fixer says it's all cool, that doesn't mean everyone agrees.

I was on edge the entire time I was in Colombia. Sicarios had told us how they carried out their hits on motorbikes, with one riding and the other on the back with a pistol. They'd pull up beside a target and fire a couple of shots, before pissing off and making the pistol disappear. (Back in London for a short break after Colombia, every time a motorbike pulled up beside my car, I'd shit myself.)

I was home for three weeks before flying out to Mexico, and Anna was away. So I booked myself on to a 10-day cookery course, to decompress. I'd been hanging out with mass murderers a few days earlier, now I was dancing around a kitchen in a chef's hat and a pinny, learning to make bread.

Having covered cocaine production in Peru and distribution in Colombia, we went to Mexico to document the violence that goes hand in hand with the cocaine trade. That meant dealing with the Sinaloa cartel, one of the largest drug-trafficking organisations in the world. Under the leadership of Joaquín 'El Chapo' Guzmán, the Sinaloa cartel became the biggest supplier of illegal drugs to the United States and unbelievably wealthy, with access to a huge arsenal of weapons. Even after El Chapo's imprisonment in 2019, the Sinaloa cartel continued to traffic hundreds of tons of cocaine from Central and South America, and kidnap, torture and kill anyone who tried to stop them.

If I'd known exactly how dangerous Mexico was, I wouldn't have gone. In 2019, the five most dangerous cities in the world, by murder rate, were all in Mexico. Culiacán, where the Sinaloa cartel are based, had slipped to twenty-first. But it's not as if it had gone soft – the cartel controls the city and the violence.

That was the year of the Battle of Culiacán, when something like 700 Sinaloa cartel battled government forces on the streets, after the Mexican National Guard captured El Chapo's son. And it's not like the Sinaloa cartel were sneaking around with pistols, they had armoured vehicles mounted with heavy machine guns, as well as rocket and grenade launchers. When the Sinaloa cartel took multiple hostages, including soldiers, the National Guard had to hand him back.

Having flown up to Culiacán from Mexico City, we made contact with our fixer and his stringers, who had organised an itinerary for us – as if he was a rep on a sightseeing holiday. The fixer went through the rules and made it clear to us that every-one knew we were there and what we we'd be doing. And when I say everyone, I mean everyone. One morning, I came down for breakfast in the hotel and the bellboy said to me, 'Good morn-ing, Mr Kane, enjoy the mountains.' That day, we were heading up to a poppy farm. It was like a scene from a gangster movie and quite unnerving. Exactly as it was meant to be.

On our first day in Culiacán, our fixer showed us a monu-ment to one of El Chapo's sons, who was gunned down on that spot by a rival cartel in 2008. Then he showed us the spot where a journalist was gunned down, for reporting on cartel violence. I think he was trying to tell us something.

Our fixer then handed us over to two local Sinaloa cartel 'PR' people, who were both off their chops on drugs and armed to the teeth. They whisked us off to interview a cartel sicario. It was night when we arrived at the safehouse, and nerves were frayed. We'd already been told that if they discovered we were being tracked, we'd be killed (and, of course, we were being). If we asked any questions other than the ones we'd already submitted, we'd be killed. If we changed any of the questions, or tried to confuse the translator, we'd be killed. One thing was abundantly clear: they had no qualms about killing us.

This safehouse was decked out like a student's bedroom, with posters of the film *Scarface* on the wall. I half expected to see one of the Mona Lisa smoking a spliff. The PR guys said the sicario would be along any minute, but he still hadn't turned up after an hour. Two hours passed, still no one. It was dark now. After about three hours, the doorbell went. Foxy opened the front door, but there was no one there. I immediately moved to the side, because I thought someone might appear and start shooting. Thankfully, nobody did. We checked the back door, but no one was there either. Just as Foxy was about to close the front door, three guys strolled in, with big old shooters and carrier bags full of cocaine.

They plonked themselves down, while we remained standing, as we'd been told to do. One of them, who was wearing a skull mask, stuck his pistol in a carrier bag, shovelled up some cocaine and snorted it from the muzzle. He was like a kid with a bag of sherbet, and he didn't stop shovelling for hours.

The translator they'd brought along was nervous as anything. Before the interview started, he told Foxy that if he disobeyed any of the rules, we'd all end up dead. He was literally begging Foxy just to ask the questions on his page and not deviate. Foxy conducted the interview standing up, face to face with one of the sicarios, right under a ceiling light. It couldn't have looked more confrontational, and that's exactly how they wanted it. Foxy was shitting himself, and I don't blame him. If anything went wrong, there was no escaping, because these boys were carrying more weaponry than an SAS patrol. At one point during the interview, one of the other guys walked over to where I was standing by the back door, pointed his pistol at my chest and waved me aside, so he could step outside for a fag. It didn't help that the translator kept making mistakes, which was pissing off the sicario no end. He kept accusing us of changing the questions and threatening to pull the plug.

After the most surreal and nerve-shredding conversation I've ever witnessed, which lasted about 20 minutes and consisted of stories of kidnapping, killing and chopping people up, we turned the camera off and the tension eased slightly. They then asked us if we wanted to see them pack a car, before driving us to a garage about 10 minutes away. This car had been completely stripped, so that every nook could be filled with millions of dollars worth of heroin. We filmed them loading it up, while they explained how they paid off guards at the various border crossing points. The guy who had pointed his pistol at me had become a bit friendlier by now (although he was still using his pistol to move us around) and even handed Foxy a slab of heroin.

After we got back to the hotel, we went straight to the bar and ordered two massive whiskies. We could have done with a bottle. I'd never been so scared for such a long period. I genuinely thought we were going to get shot when Foxy opened the door of that safehouse. And we were with those guys for six or seven hours, while they were getting higher and higher. I wondered why I was there. What was the point of it? Dying while trying to do something that had never been done before made some kind of sense to me. Getting bumped off by a hitman for a drug cartel in Mexico for being a bit nosy, didn't.

But there was no backing out now. I'd promised to be there for Foxy and that was the end of it. The following day, we were scheduled to visit the Sinaloa cartel's security detail, a rogue guerrilla group based about an hour and a half outside Culiacán. Their job is to patrol the outskirts, keep the cops at bay and ensure Culiacán remains a Sinaloa stronghold. On the way out there, we were waved through three or four police checkpoints, without a single awkward question being asked.

After a while we pulled off the main road and followed a sand track down to a lake, shielded by a hill and surrounded by trees with a river running off it. There were a couple of pickups on the other side of the lake and about eight Sinaloa guerrillas milling about decked out in paramilitary uniforms and carrying AK-47s and radios. A guy paddled us over in a canoe, Foxy and the director on the first trip, me and the filming kit on the second.

The commander, who we were there to interview, was very charismatic. He had a big scar on his hand from when someone had tried to shoot him at close quarters, and he'd put his hand over the end of the pistol. Before the interview started, he told us the Mexican marines had just left their base and were heading this way. When I asked how he knew this, he replied, 'We've got people everywhere.'

Sure enough, about 30 minutes later, we started to hear helicopters carrying out counter-narco patrols. In Mexico, the marines are the only security force not on the cartels' payrolls and the only one the US Drug Enforcement Administration (DEA) trusts when it's carrying out anti-narco operations. When the choppers came into view, the guerrillas disappeared into the bushes, leaving Foxy, the cameraman, the director and me sitting out in the open. As the choppers flew off, the guerrillas reappeared and the interview continued.

Like every narco we spoke to, the commander revelled in his evil. When Foxy asked him if there was anything he hadn't done, the commander fixed Foxy with a wicked stare and replied, 'I'm yet to kill a Western journalist', before throwing his head back, laughing manically and patting Foxy on the back. Just then, a helicopter appeared in the distance, flying a few metres above the water, scattering the guerrillas for a second time. As the helicopter flew past, we could see the marines looking straight at us. When the commander popped up again, he told us what we already knew, that we had been compromised and the interview was over. Soon, the marines would be back in force and there would be a gun fight.

The canoe guy paddled Foxy, the camera operator and the director back across, leaving me behind. And suddenly a cartoon-like storm arrived. It went from typical steamy Mexican heat to icy cold in a matter of seconds, and the rain started coming down so hard I could barely see Foxy, the director, camera operator or the canoe guy on the other side of the lake. I had to jump into the back of a pickup with the guerrillas, who promptly started chopping up cocaine on the dashboard and hoovering it up.

They were absolutely terrified of lightning so the situation couldn't have been much worse. I was stuck in the middle of a storm with eight nervous cartel guerrillas carrying AK–47s and off their heads on cocaine. And the boss had just been talking about killing a Western journalist. My mates were on the other side of a lake, a unit of marines was on its way, our escape route was already a river of sand and our getaway car was two-wheel drive.

Then, as quickly as the storm started, it stopped. The canoe guy paddled across, took me back over and Foxy started explaining how he'd almost been fried by a bolt of lightning. It had missed him by a few metres, and he was white as a sheet.

It was about 4.8 kilometres to the main road and the car was just about managing it until we rounded a bend and came across a fallen tree. On the other side of the tree were eight Humvees with top guns containing 60 or 70 marines armed to the teeth.

The commander was not happy with us, but after we'd showed him our press accreditation there was nothing he could do. The marines cut through the tree with chainsaws, jumped back on the Humvees and streamed past. That was going to be a one-sided fight, if they could find the guerrillas.

This gig was getting hairier and hairier by the day and no amount of whiskey was taking the edge off. There was danger everywhere, even when the Sinaloa cartel were nowhere to be seen. We were driving to lunch one day when our driver pulled out right in front of a rusty banger driven by a little old guy wearing a sombrero, with what appeared to be a rolled-up shop shutter tied to the top. The banger braked hard, hit us and drilled us across two lanes of the highway. We were all okay, but when I got out of our Landcruiser, I noticed the shop shutter had flown off the banger like a javelin and gone straight through our rear window, decapitating the head rest directly behind mine. If the old guy had been going a few miles per hour faster, the shop shutter would have taken my head off.

The poor director went into shock and was literally shaking. I saw the irony: we'd been hanging out with some of the most dangerous men in Mexico and lived to tell the tale, and now I'd almost been decapitated by a flying shop shutter. When I pointed out to Foxy that I'd almost died, he replied, 'Yeah, but you fucking didn't . . .' Oh to have Foxy's simple logic.

It felt safer in the mountains, where we travelled to film heroin production in the poppy fields. The guys there seemed like simple farming folk and were happy to take us through the ropes, showing us how they cut the poppies and collected the gum, which is then turned into heroin. But on the second evening, I entered our safehouse in the village and the two fixers were sitting there ashen-faced. They said there was nothing to worry about, but I could tell they were lying. If we were in trouble, I needed to make plans, so I kept digging. Eventually one of them told me, 'They're coming to get us.'

That day, we'd originally arranged to visit a crack lab, to film it being made. But the director had cancelled, saying Foxy was ill. Because the Sinaloa cartel have eyes and ears everywhere, they knew Foxy wasn't ill and that we were filming up in the mountains instead. The PR guys were incensed. It didn't matter that we were filming with another branch of the cartel, what mattered was that we'd lied to them. We were deep in Sinaloa country, with Sinaloa people. And now we had a different bunch of Sinaloa people coming after us. I was utterly terrified.

I woke Foxy up and told him the bad news, before phoning London and telling the Secret Compass team that we needed to get the hell out of Mexico. None of us slept that night. I kept picturing a couple of pickups trundling up the mountain, crammed full of sicarios. At first light, we jumped in our cars and hightailed it back down to Culiacán. Mercifully, we didn't pass any sicarios on the way. A couple of hours later, we were on a plane to Mexico City.

By this stage, I really felt like we were pushing our luck. I wanted to go home, but we had one last place on our itinerary. Had someone asked me to visit Acapulco 20 years ago, I would have jumped at the chance. Once upon a time, it was a popular holiday resort, mostly associated with American students on spring break. But not many tourists visit nowadays. For the last decade or so, rival drug cartels have battled on Acapulco's streets, cops and politicians have been bumped off, and headless bodies dumped on main thoroughfares.

It was too dangerous to work with the bad guys in Acapulco, because there was something like 50 competing cartels, so we hung out with the good guys instead. (We'd avoided working with the cops elsewhere, because if they'd suddenly hit the bad guys, they would have assumed we'd tipped them off and killed us.)

We spent two days filming with a forensic scientist, whose job was to identify – or try to identify – all these bodies that kept popping up. A couple of days earlier, a body had washed up on the beach. This scientist insisted on showing us videos of cartel victims, which wasn't great for Foxy's PTSD (I didn't look, because those things you can't unsee). Apparently there were people hanging from bridges, people with their penises cut off, people whose insides had been eaten by dogs, while they were still alive. One video showed the name of a cartel spelled out with a victim's entrails. He also took us to the city morgue, which contained scores of unidentified bodies, or bits of them. The fridges weren't working, so we could smell it from a couple of blocks away. It was the worst sightseeing tour I'd ever been on.

Only after I'd returned to London did I fully appreciate how lucky we'd been. The toughest part of the job was that we were always in danger, even when it didn't seem like it. The cartels had eyes all over Colombia and Mexico, always knew where we were and what we were doing. In hindsight, we were less likely to have been killed by a hardened sicario than by an ambitious, coked-up teenager, wanting to prove his minerals and make us his trophy.

People sometimes ask if I enjoy danger – if I find it 'fun'. Well, there are different types of fun. There's easy fun – or what I call 'type-one fun' – which is the enjoyment you get from playing a game or having a laugh with your mates down the pub. Then there's 'type-two fun', which is the deeper sense of enjoyment you get from abseiling into a volcano or rowing the Atlantic.

'Type-two fun' comes from the satisfaction of the graft something takes to achieve and the camaraderie it engenders with your 'team'. It's being cold, wet through and broken. It's gasping for air, craving food, with mega blisters on your feet and chafing between your legs. It might not seem 'fun' at the time but you look back on it with great fondness and humour, even if you almost die! That South American trip was 'type-three fun': it wasn't enjoyable at the time and it still isn't looking back on it. I got some decent stories out of it, but I'd never do it again. Unless of course, Foxy asked me to . . .

CHAPTER 12

Lockdown: Make the Best of Your Situation

If I'd been with someone other than Anna, these months would have been a severe test of our relationship. Between flying out to Peru in July and returning home from Mexico in October, we'd managed to see each other once, when we grabbed two hours together at Heathrow as we flew in different directions. And about a month and a half later, I was flying off to Rwanda, recceing a Netflix film called *This Is Football*, about how the sport was used as a recovery and reconciliatory tool after the genocide, among other things.

That trip brought a pretty stressful 2017 to an end and I managed to spend time with Anna over Christmas and New Year (she'd been travelling around the Equator with Scottish filmmaker Gordon Buchanan, so was in need of some downtime as well). Not that 2018 was going to be any calmer.

After a couple of months off, I was in Russia and Ukraine for another Guy Martin documentary – and Guy always manages to pack a lot into a four-week shoot.

And two days after getting home from Ukraine, I flew out to Borneo to pit my wits against the explorer Ed Stafford. It was for Ed's new Discovery show *Ed Stafford: First Man Out*, which would pit him against six survival experts in six different settings, racing to complete a journey with minimal provisions. When they first asked me to do it, I wasn't sure I wanted to. I had plenty of other work in the diary and wasn't sure I needed to ruin myself for public entertainment. But then I thought, 'I'm always on social media, banging on about being this tough-guy adventurer. When was the last time I actually tested myself?'

The best part of my job is getting to work in different environments with different types of people. But the longer I go without challenging myself, doing something that tests me to the limit, I start to question myself. Am I *really* that dude that people think I am? Or have I lost it? After some humming and hawing, I got on the phone to Ed and said, 'I'm happy to do it. I don't care if you beat me, I just want to test myself.'

Ed became famous when he became the first person to walk the length of the Amazon, which took him over two years. Along the way, he got held up at gunpoint and by bow and arrow and arrested for drug smuggling and murder. He'd also done a TV series called *Marooned with Ed Stafford*, which involved him being dropped in remote locations, with no clothes, food or tools, and trying to survive for however long. Like me, he'd been a Scout and served in the military. He was going to be a formidable opponent. Just not as formidable as the mangrove swamps of Sepilok, situated near Sandakan, up in the Malaysian part of Borneo.

Mangrove swamps are one of the most difficult, hostile environments you can work in. The water isn't fresh, it's salty – so you can't drink it. The mangrove roots are a nightmare, millions of them, as thick as your legs, hiding under the water and waiting to snap your bones or trap you. Then there are the tides to consider. The tide comes in twice a day and you can get marooned on a small section of swamp. And if you try to swim, you're taking your life in your hands, because there are some of the biggest saltwater crocodiles on earth lurking everywhere.

On reflection, probably only Ed Stafford could have thought this was a good idea.

After arriving in Sandakan, Ed and I spent two days practising skills – making fire, sharpening sticks, whittling spoons, the sort of bushcraft I've loved since my Scouting days. After those few days I really got to know Ed and liked him, he was a deeply motivated human and one of my own kind. The race would last for seven days, from point A to point B. We'd have no help from production crews but both have a cameraman assigned to us.

At first, I couldn't understand how the cameramen would keep up with us. But when I was told my cameraman, a guy called Joe French, was a member of Loch Abber Rescue and an absolute beast of a fell runner, I started worrying that I might not be able to keep up with him. Those people are ninjas, because they do almost everything the person on your screen is doing while filming, often backwards, with a heavy camera. It's like that Ginger Rogers quote: 'I did everything Fred Astaire did, but backwards and in high heels.' (Just to be clear, Joe didn't wear high heels in the swamp.)

The race started with us being driven to within about 100 metres of the swamp and pointed in a rough direction. Then someone counted us down – 'Three! Two! One!' – and we were off, heading north. Seconds after wading in, I had to go back and free Joe's legs, because he was up to his knees in mud with his camera and bag weighing him down. When darkness descended, all I could think about was being grabbed by a croc, dragged under, death-rolled and chopped to pieces. I really did think about it in that much detail. I had a knife, but if the croc saw me first, I wouldn't have a chance. I'd be halfway inside him in just one bite, their jaws are really that big.

At one point during the first 24 hours, I built a balancing pole to get up onto a big branch that was arched over the swamp. I was utterly ball-bagged already. I was drenched and starving (Joe could eat, I couldn't!) with leeches hanging off every part of my body. And just as I started doing this piece to camera about the water beneath me being full of man-eating crocs, the branch snapped. If the crocs didn't know I was there before that, they did now.

I knew I had to build my shelters above the high tide mark, but when you've been wading through swamp for the previous 12 hours on no food or drink, your mind stops working properly and you make mistakes. The first time I made a shelter, I chopped down some branches, created a platform and bent some leaves over the top, like an orangutan nest. I was convinced it was high enough, but almost as soon as it got dark, I could feel water lapping around me. It was only about a foot below my platform, which meant I didn't sleep a wink. Every time I closed my eyes, I pictured a croc torpedoing out of the water and dragging me under. Had that happened, no one would have known, because Joe was sleeping in a hammock up on higher ground.

I didn't see Ed for about four or five days. I did hear him calling my name at one point, but didn't reply. I was in game mode and wasn't going to betray my position. I laid low for an hour, let him pass through and dog-legged out of his way. And once I got used to the privation, I started to enjoy it, in the weird way that I do.

Ed wanted me to demonstrate fieldcraft on camera, which was right up my street. One day, I made a nine-metre rope, with a grappling hook at the end, out of rattan and some mangrove root spikes (the roots are covered with those things, and they rip your legs to shreds). I stood on one side of the river, threw it across and it wrapped around some branches and locked into

184

place. I then attached the other end to a tree, pulled it tight and monkeyed my way over.

Admittedly, the food wasn't great. Over the seven days, the only things I ate were two sea slugs and a crab. I had to dig around in the mud to find those sea slugs and they tasted as rancid as you'd imagine – they were bright green and covered in mucus. As I was chewing on them, I thought, 'I am definitely going to die of some horrendous disease.' The crab, which I caught in a rattan trap, wasn't much better. Crab meat is lovely when it's cooked, but looks, feels and tastes like sludge when it's not.

It probably helped that I didn't care if I won or not. For Ed, winning was kind of the point. He had this reputation as a crack survivalist and would have looked a bit daft if he'd lost all the races. But I was just cracking on, pushing north and doing everything to the best of my ability. So it came as a bit of a surprise after six days when I came across one of Ed's camps, with the ash from the fire still hot. I was a bit irritated, because I hadn't been able to get a fire going. But that's Ed's thing, he could start a fire underwater, and I now knew I was right on his heels. And that's when my competitive spirit kicked in.

I stole some ash from his fire, which meant I was finally able to make my own fire later on. That I did by making a fire roll, which involved rubbing tinder and ash between some wood. That cranked things up a level. I was delirious, cramping up, tripping all over the place and screaming and swearing at Joe, but the competitive spirit had totally consumed me. The finish point was an orangutan viewing platform in Sepilok Nature Resort, and by the time we arrived I was broken and deflated, because I was sure Ed was already there. It was only after I'd climbed a six-metre ladder to reach the top of the platform that I discovered I'd won.

I actually felt quite sad, because I'd wanted Ed to win. But me winning served a purpose. That was the first episode they filmed, and it showed that Ed could be beaten at his own game and it wasn't rigged. (Ed, who's become a good mate, was pissed off, but it put a rocket up his arse and meant he didn't lose the next one!) For me, it was more about proving that I still had it in me. That night, Ed and I got happily drunk. And when my head hit my pillow, I didn't think, 'When was the last time I did something hard?' Instead, I thought, 'Maybe I am still that dude.'

Two days later, I was back in Mexico, working on another expedition with Steve Backshall. This was the first shoot for a new series of 10 expeditions aiming to be world firsts. (The opening sequence to this film was me and Steve carrying heavy loads into the jungle. My eyes were hollow, and I was struggling with the weight as I was still recovering from not having eaten or slept properly for a week in Borneo.)

My official job was safety person and expedition leader, but I was also Steve's on-camera buddy. The 'first' on this trip was a dive into an underwater cave system under the Yucatán Peninsula, on the Caribbean coast. There's a massive 150-kilometres-long crater on the coast there that some scientists think was made by the meteor that wiped out the dinosaurs 66 million years ago. (Although, I should point out, some scientists don't think the dinosaurs were wiped out by a meteor at all.) The cave system (a freshwater system called an aquifer) is thought to be the longest on the planet, at 347 kilometres, and was of great importance to the Mayans, to whom it was an underworld for their gods.

The cave system is made up of cenotes, or sinkholes, which are full of turquoise water, stalagmites and stalactites (which may have symbolised penises in Mayan culture). We used hundreds of

Me and Foxy taking a break towards the end of our record-setting 50-day row across the Atlantic. 2016.

Me and Ross Johnson on the oars of *Ellida*. Team Essence mainland to mainland expedition in 2016 where we became the first team ever to row from mainland Europe to mainland South America.

The camera team filming the lava lake at night from our campsite, inside the volcano. The largest lava lake on earth truly does come to life at night. 2016.

Climbing back out from Tier 2 after a long day rigging and filming. The climb out used over 2 kilometres of rope strung out over the volcano like spider webs. *Expedition Volcano*, 2017.

My third expedition into Nyiragongo volcano and the first time I was able to make it to the very bottom. Shortly after this photo was taken, the entire tier above where I was standing collapsed. 2017.

Picking my way through the ice flow in Scoresby Sound, Greenland with Steve Backshall just days after surfacing from the nuclear bunker experiment. *Expedition*, 2018.

Discussing the merits of using human poo as fertiliser in China with Guy Martin. *Our Guy in China,* 2018.

Weaving a vine rope in the mangroves of Borneo going head-to-head against Ed Stafford in *First Man Out,* 2018. Photo Rob Sixsmith.

The biggest abseil I have ever rigged. A single-drop overhanging 400-metre abseil off the waterfall at Jebel Shams in Oman. Steve Backshall and I tentatively drop into the canyon to explore further. 2018.

The big day. My brothers and sister at our wedding. Struan, me, Anna, Stroma, Ross and Ruairidh. 2019.

Me and Will Smith inside Mount Yasur volcano, Tanna Island. *Welcome to Earth*, 2019.

Rigging and testing the system that we would use to get Will Smith into the moulin in Iceland. 2020.

Filming with the Dinka people of South Sudan. We had to cut the filming mission short and fly straight back into national lockdown due to the coronavirus outbreak. 2020.

Dive preparation for *OceanXplorers* series, shaking out my rebreather unit. 2021. Photo Katy Fraser.

Watching Anna give birth while on expedition in the Atlantic Ocean.
Atlas was born 17 days before I returned. The sacrifice of a life of adventure.
Our family: Anna, Atlas and our dog Hector.

metres of rope to get down there, but the Mayans must have slithered in without any support whatsoever, naked and carrying burning torches. At the bottom of one cenote, we discovered 20-odd skulls, belonging to cows and humans, young and adult. These were possibly Mayan sacrifices, made for their gods before the arrival of the Spanish in the sixteenth century. After seven or eight hours of exploring, we discovered new passages containing Mayan cave art, including stencilled handprints and depictions of the jaguar god of the underworld. In one passage, there was an altar and smashed pots on the cardinal points of a compass. This was spine-tingling, full-on Indiana Jones stuff, seeing things that hadn't been seen for thousands of years and bringing an ancient civilisation back from the dead (thanks to our amazing local scientist and real-life Indy – Guillermo De Anda).

I really needed a nice relaxing break after that trip. Between flying out to Russia on 21 March and flying home from Mexico on 22 May, I'd spent two days in my own bed. The flat was a wreck. There was kit strewn everywhere: duvet jackets from my time in Siberia, jungle books, knives and machetes from Borneo, ropes, diving kit and all my climbing gear from my trip to Mexico. But I barely had time to tidy the place up before disappearing inside a bunker for 10 days. They didn't even let me take my faithful hoover in with me.

By this point in my TV career, I'd earned a reputation as an ex-military man who'd done lots of challenging things and was able to talk about them without swearing too much. I think that's why BBC Two's *Horizon* team asked me to take part in a documentary called *Body Clock: What Makes Us Tick?*

Their idea was to stick me in a confined space with no daylight, so that scientists could study how my circadian rhythms (the internal process that regulates a person's sleep–wake cycle) would be affected by a lack of daylight over a prolonged period. You might think that sounds a bit extreme, but as the scientists pointed out, the way most people live their lives today is extreme from an evolutionary perspective. Human beings are animals, and not really meant to be stuck in dark offices with artificial light for hours on end. And we all live by the same clock, even though not everyone's circadian rhythms are the same.

Scientists had already proved that altering our circadian rhythms can be bad for our health (studies on shift workers show that if we regularly disrupt our sleep, we're at greater risk of diabetes, heart disease and cancer). So understanding them is quite important. But scientists also knew that being stuck in a confined space with no light could drive people out of their minds.

I'd seen documentaries about people who had spent years in solitary confinement and they were scarred for life. In America, many death row prisoners are kept in solitary confinement for years on end, and if they're not mad when they go in, they often are by the time they're executed. Meanwhile, the United Nations considers solitary confinement exceeding 15 days as torture. All in all, it sounded pretty grim. But I was supposed to be this tough guy, that was my 'thing', so I didn't really think I could say no. Again, I was keen to test myself.

They originally planned to keep me in a cave, but a few days before I was supposed to go in, I asked the producer if they'd checked it for gases. When they did, they discovered large quantities of radon, which is a colourless, odourless, radioactive gas. Had I spent 10 days in that cave, it might have done me permanent damage. The producer found a nuclear bunker in Devon instead. It made no real difference to me.

On arrival, I was led down three flights of stairs into a small, damp room containing a camp bed, a set of shelves, a bucket to do my business in, a microwave and 10 microwavable meals, plus an inflatable paddling pool, a jerrycan (a water transporter) with a pump and a hose handle for washing. The room was also rigged with cameras, like on *Big Brother*, which would capture me doing various experiments. These included arithmetic tests, grip tests and games (I had one of those steady hand buzzer toys, with the metal wand and twisted wire, to test my co-ordination, and flashing discs on the wall, to test my reactions). I'd do a suite of six experiments seven times a day, to see how my body was reacting and if my brain was becoming less agile as time went on.

This room was completely soundproofed, so that when the TV people and scientists left, locking the door behind them, the sound of silence was deafening. It was so quiet I could literally hear my heartbeat. For the first hour or so, I just sat on my bed, in the dark, wondering – not for the first time in my life – what I'd got myself into. Anna had just flown out to Brazil to chase illegal loggers in the Amazon, and I thought that's what I should have been doing. Or at least something like that. Instead, I'd volunteered for a solid stretch in solitary confinement, something that hardened prisoners dread.

I was allowed to take in a couple of sets of clothes, a washbag and a few books, that was it. I had no watch or electronics, other than a production camera (with the time stamp disabled) attached to a tripod for filming short video diary entries. There were a few 10-watt bulbs in the room (to aid filming), so I could just about make things out. But I couldn't read my books (my only luxury) without switching my head torch on.

The first thing I did was draw 10 squares on the wall, each one denoting a day I would be down there. In my everyday life,

I use a diary and wall planner, which help me keep an organised, disciplined routine. I thought those 10 squares would maybe have the same effect. I used up half an hour trying to fathom how the microwave worked (I'd never used one before!) and was amazed that it could cook a curry in five minutes. After a feed, I read for about an hour, walked around the room for a bit, did a few press-ups and then thought, 'Bloody hell, I'm bored already.' Luckily, I was exhausted from just returning from the cave diving expedition with Steve in Mexico a day or so prior, so fell asleep quite easily.

I soon realised that diaries, wall planners or squares drawn on a wall become irrelevant when you don't know what time of day it is. I thought I'd be able to keep rough track of time through my sleep cycles, crossing off a square every time I awoke from what I thought had been decent kip. But I didn't actually know how many hours I'd got, because I had no idea what time I'd gone to bed or woken up. People used to judge what time to go to bed and wake up by the position of the sun and how dark or light it was. Modern people have clocks to aid them. And most of them know how much sleep they need, so they slip into a routine, going to bed and waking up at roughly the same time every day. But if you're deprived of daylight and a clock, everything goes haywire. By day two, I was already disorientated and starting to unravel.

I tried to use the experiments as a rough guide to the passing of time, drawing the numbers one to seven on the wall and ticking them off as I did them. In between the experiments, I read. It was all about trying to create a routine. One of the books I brought in was called *Why Time Flies* by Alan Burdick, because I wanted to learn about the concept of time. But time certainly didn't fly in the bunker. A minute felt like an hour and an hour felt like an eternity. At least I think they did.

190

By day three, I was struggling to even read. I honestly can't remember anything about *Why Time Flies*, because my concentration was shot to pieces. People fantasise about being imprisoned and putting their time to good use – studying, learning chess, law, a musical instrument, languages – and coming out a genius. But my mind was all over the place and I couldn't hold on to a train of thought. Sometimes, I'd be thinking about lots of different things at once. Other times, I'd find myself just staring at the wall. When I'd snap out of it, I'd have no idea if I'd been staring at the wall for three minutes or 30.

I spent a lot of time in the bunker talking to myself. I do that a lot in the real world, as a way of dealing with stressful situations (I might be setting up an abseil and find myself talking to the rigging), but not as much as this. Because there was no other noise, it felt like talking to someone else. After recording a diary entry, I'd switch my camera off and be overwhelmed by sadness, as if someone had just left the room. A few times, I found myself picking the video camera up and looking behind it. But there was never anyone there.

I started to lose track of reality and become paranoid. I'd think, 'Are they messing with me? Am I ever getting out?' In hindsight, it was ridiculous to be thinking like that. Of course I was getting out, it was a BBC television programme. But that just goes to show what solitary confinement can do to someone. Imagine being banged up in a cell and not having any idea when you are going to be released, if ever. Many hostages have been through exactly that, including Terry Waite, who was captured by Islamist militants in Lebanon in 1987 and held in solitary confinement for four years. It's difficult to comprehend just how strong that man's mind must be.

After four or five days, I'd completely forgotten about the
cameras. I was pulling my pants down and going to the toilet,
getting my kit off and washing, and it didn't even occur to me
that there were a load of TV people and scientists watching.
That's what happens when you're put in a position like that, you
slowly lose any sense of dignity. I even stopped doing press-ups.
I just couldn't be arsed. I'd consider doing them and then think,
'What's the point?' But what was I going to do instead? I never
sleep during the day. Once I'm up, that's it. When I work from
home, I won't even go into the living room, let alone lie on
the couch and take a nap. I thought that would help me in the
bunker, in that I wouldn't just sleep on and off but would keep
to some kind of rhythm. But once time starts slipping, and you
don't know what time you're going to bed or how long you're
sleeping for, you just feel fatigued all the time.

Every organ in your body has its own circadian rhythm,
working on a cycle that varies between 24 and 26 hours (the
scientists worked out that my full circadian rhythm was about 25
hours and 15 minutes). But when you're deprived of daylight,
your circadian rhythm doesn't get reset and your body goes into
freefall. I was going to bed an hour later every day, and despite
getting five or six hours' sleep, I was waking up feeling absolutely terrible.

After seven or eight days, I was apparently going to bed at
about 5am. And by that stage, they'd started to really mess with
my head. They'd told me beforehand that they were going to
gradually introduce sleep deprivation, which involved sounding
a siren at some point during my sleep. I'd get up, do a set of
experiments and fall back into bed, before going through the
same routine an hour later. After the third siren, which had a
different sound, I'd know to remain awake. Once they started

deliberately disrupting my sleep, my performances in the experiments took a nosedive. That was the scientists demonstrating how important a regular sleep pattern is and how jetlag can wreak havoc. My body was completely out of sync; I was active when I should have been resting and resting when my body should have been active.

After nine days – or what I thought was nine days – it was all getting a bit much. I was convinced I'd miscounted, kept wondering how long I had left. I remember thinking, 'Am I getting out of here today or is it tonight? I'm not sure how much longer I can do this.' In the documentary, I'm shown roaring in frustration. I hadn't seen daylight, exercised or chatted to anyone for far longer than was healthy and my mental health was beginning to suffer. On a basic level, I was really, really bored. But it was much more than that.

I was still vaguely in control and just about able to make sense of things. I kept saying to myself, 'This won't last forever. I have not been taken hostage and thrown in a dungeon. It will end soon.' That's why a more effective experiment (if not an ethical one) would have been to put me in there without telling me when I was getting out. That would have played on one of people's biggest fears, that of the unknown. I reckon it would have been crushing, physically and emotionally. Even as it was, a few more days inside might have had me clawing the walls and bashing my head against the door.

Mercifully, a couple of hours later I heard the door being unlocked and the film crew streamed in. They gave me a big pair of sunglasses and led me outside. I felt like Dorothy from *The Wizard of Oz*, suddenly switching from black and white to glorious technicolour. Because I'd been in a sound-proof room for 10 days, I could hone in on the slightest noise. I could hear bees flying. I could taste pollen and smell decomposing vegetation. I felt like I could almost see the scent coming off the grass, flowers and trees. (I was reminded of how it felt to reach dry land after the ocean row.) It was an incredibly profound moment, being reacquainted with all the wonderful things that people too often take for granted. I thought, 'Make the most of this, because it could all be gone at the flick of a switch.' I felt powerful, as if I could do anything. Which, of course, had a lot of truth to it. Then I thought, 'Jesus, all these people have seen me shitting in a bucket.'

While the scientists had put me in the bunker to study circadian rhythms, my biggest takeaway had to do with mental health. Mental health is the same as physical health, in that you need to work at it. Of course, being stuck in a small room with no company or sunlight for 10 days is an extreme situation, but the more extreme a situation, the greater insight it can give you. Naturally, daylight is crucial for mental health. But to keep mental illness at bay, you must also keep yourself busy and nourish your brain. Humans haven't evolved to sit around all day doing nothing, or staring at a TV, phone or computer screen. They should be active and out in the real world. And being social creatures, people should not be on their own for extended periods.

During the coronavirus lockdowns, I did a load of interviews about my time in the bunker, because people thought the situations were analogous. They were right to a certain extent. Like my bunker experiment, lockdown involved people being cooped up for days on end against their will. (Admittedly, I didn't have to do the bunker experiment, and could have tapped out at any time; but once I was in there, there was no way I was leaving early.) In both scenarios, the best way to get through it was by creating a routine and sticking to it. Routine and discipline were what got me through the bunker experience, kept me on the straight and narrow and gave me a kick up the arse. I'm not saying it was easy to stick to, and I discarded some of the things I planned to do quite early on – if the 'why' isn't big enough then you'll never get motivated to do it, not even in lockdown. Just the existence of a routine provides a focus. It gives you a solid foundation, and if you don't have a solid foundation, you'll spend your days stumbling and fumbling as if on sand.

When some people hear the word 'discipline', they automatically think it's a bad thing – boring and anti-fun. The Marines definitely cemented routine and discipline as part of my life, but even as a child I had understood that one step in front of the other and the discipline to follow through can take you anywhere.

Lockdown was hard for so many people because the discipline they previously had in their lives was imposed by other people and 'accepted' practices: for example, if you have to be at work by a certain time, your routine is dictated by your company/boss, not you. Life is difficult if you're suddenly stuck at home with no one telling you what to do, and where to be. That's when it's easy to end up sitting around in your pants, eating crap food because you can't be bothered to cook, not washing, not doing anything and wondering where the week has gone. Sitting down and making a plan, breaking your waking hours into chunks and trying to achieve something within each chunk makes the days pass a lot quicker.

But while I did see certain similarities between the bunker experiment and lockdown, some of the lockdown chat baffled me. I was listening to all the doom and gloom and thinking, 'Am I missing something?' Yes, I, along with many others, lost a year's worth of income almost overnight (and I fell through all of the government help schemes) but I knew that life would return to normal at some point. We had to stay indoors most of the time, but we could see daylight, turn a tap on, exercise or take the dog for a walk, pick up the phone and talk to mates, read books, surf the internet, learn things, pop out for food or have it delivered to the door. During the first lockdown, I had a parcel delivery almost every day!

Obviously, it wasn't that simple for those battling illness, loss or financial/job pressures. And unlike the bunker experiment, we didn't know when lockdown was going to end. Many struggled with anxiety and mental health issues (especially in the winter, which was the case with the second extended lockdown) and sheer loneliness at the separation from loved ones and social interaction. I also think that lockdown brought some people face to face with their real selves and life choices, and they didn't like what they saw.

Instead of making people feel even more miserable, I recommended tools they could use. Nothing complicated, just practical advice, like getting up early (which I know is a real battle for some people), having a shower, making your bed, getting dressed and drawing up a list of things to do. If you manage to do all that before a decent hour is up, and then put that list into action, your day will probably be more bearable. Planning days to the letter during uncertain times also keeps you focused on and locked in the present – which is the most important time and the only time you have full control over – rather than worrying about the future or the past. If you could get some exercise in before breakfast, all the better. Knowing that you've already got the hardest part of the day out of the way makes everything else seem easier, and just the sound of the dawn chorus, a reminder of nature's permanence, can be tremendously uplifting.

I also advised people not to turn the TV on until the evening and to disengage from the news because most of it was bad; and also to eat healthily, because that's just common sense. My final advice was to cut down on social media. For one, social media is mainly people arguing about that bad news, which is just depressing. And it's also the greatest thief of time ever invented. I use it to get my message out there but it's designed to be addictive, so that you're constantly feeding it and looking to it for affirmation, mainly from strangers. Instead of staring at a screen all day and aimlessly swiping, I advised people to contact those they actually knew, which was easier than ever during lockdown with Zoom and all the other communication apps. Speaking to an old mate you've lost contact with or making a special effort to speak to a vulnerable relative can make someone's day.

I always feel like I'm underachieving, as if I could be doing more, so I viewed lockdown as an opportunity. Like everyone else, I had 24 hours to play with each day. But I didn't waste time or stew. I always make the best of whatever situation I'm in. When I'm in a cave in Borneo, eating my freeze-dried eggs and beans, I'm not thinking, 'I wish this was steak and chips.' Sitting around thinking about all the other stuff you could be doing is not good for the mind or the soul. What lockdown gave me was lots of spare time, and you can use spare time to learn things and make plans.

Straight after my release from the bunker, I had to do an interview for the documentary – and it had to be a quick one, because I was flying to Greenland that same evening for another of Steve Backshall's *Expedition* series. I hadn't really thought all this through. Unfortunately, the interview overran by 15 minutes, and the researcher who'd been tasked with ferrying me to Plymouth train station got stuck behind a tractor.

Having lived without time, daylight or people for the previous 10 days, I suddenly found myself running through the station, eyes glued to the clock, terrified that time would defeat me. So it turned out. As I reached the platform, the whistle sounded, followed by beeping and the train doors closing.

I said to the guard, 'Mate, I really needed to be on that train.'

'You're late.'

'I've been in a bunker for 10 days!'

'We don't wait for anyone.'

Oh, the irony.

The next train wasn't for ages, so I jumped in a taxi to Bristol (which cost £180), caught a train from Bristol to Paddington and the Tube from Paddington to Tooting, where I was now living with Anna. I had to pack my Arctic kit and finish prepping for my next trip quickly before 6pm, when a taxi picked me up to whisk me to Heathrow. Two taxis, one train, two planes, one helicopter and 10 hours after getting out of the bunker, I was in Ittoqqortoormiit, Eastern Greenland. That's what you call a shock to the system.

CHAPTER 13

Hunting the Traffickers: Challenge Yourself

By 2016 I had worked on many productions, but I always felt I could be using my skills in a more worthwhile way working in TV. I had seen first-hand the vital work of the rangers in Virunga National Park, and knew how under-resourced the fight against poaching was, so I started to talk to production companies and commissioners about ideas that mattered.

My first conservation production was a show-and-tell film with Foxy in South Africa for the charity Veterans For Wildlife, which had asked me and Foxy to be ambassadors. Veterans For Wildlife helps soldiers who have suffered PTSD or mental health issues from fighting in Iraq and Afghanistan (which Foxy had been quite vocal about), taking them to Africa to train rangers in first aid, anti-ambush and contact drills and how to set up patrols. It kills two birds with one stone, giving former soldiers renewed purpose and showing them how the skills they've learned are relevant to the world outside the military, as well as helping in the fight against illegal poaching.

Foxy and I visited sanctuaries where adult rhinos that had survived attacks were kept, as well as baby orphaned rhinos suffering with PTSD. We went on patrol with the rangers, who are regularly killed by poachers and get paid next to nothing. I was baffled by the state of their kit. There were all these high-profile wildlife charities making millions of pounds each year and those at the heart of fighting poaching, the rangers on the ground, were walking around in boots that were falling apart. They had old weapons and were only given one meal a day.

We took new boots, compasses and rucksacks over but those on the ground needed much more than that. If I ran a charity whose stated aim was to save rhinos or elephants, the first job on my list would be to provide those rangers with the best weapons, cameras and drones. Offer a Marine the option of an extra £20 a month or the best boots on the market, and they'll take the boots every time.

While on patrol at one of the national parks, we heard gunshots and came across a rhino that had recently been mown down and hacked up. It had been shot two or three times in the face, stomach and chest – the poachers had probably sawn its horn off while it was still breathing. They wanted as much of the horn as possible, so had taken the whole of the front of the animal's face off. That rhino's horn would already be on its way to Mozambique, or somewhere else on the east coast of Africa, from where it would be trafficked to Asia. And the same traffickers, using the same routes, would also be smuggling cheetah cubs and skins to the Middle East, as well as minerals, gold, weapons and humans to all corners of the globe.

Seeing that dead rhino broke my heart. And that was just one rhino of thousands that had been slaughtered in the same way. Only 60 years ago, rhinos were relatively common in Africa. Now there are only about 20,000 southern white rhinos remaining, 5,000 black rhinos and only two northern white rhinos, both in captivity and both female, which means the subspecies is functionally extinct.

I've always had a huge interest in wildlife. When I was a kid, I was in a Young Ornithologist club, as well as being fascinated by animals big and small. Wildlife conservation was a complicated subject, but the poaching situation in South Africa was on a whole different level. The poachers are doing the actual killing, but they're risking their lives, hoping not to get eaten by lions or leopards or shot by rangers, because they're right at the bottom of the economic ladder, and struggling to look after themselves and their families (exactly the same as the guys at the bottom of the narco chains, the farmers and the growers, etc.).

It's those higher up the food chain who are the problem, including the consumers, wealthy people mainly in China, who think powdered rhino horn can cure them of a variety of ailments despite there being little scientific evidence to back up their beliefs. That's the reason wildlife crime is one of the most lucrative criminal activities, after the drugs trade and human trafficking.

Rhino horn is just the tip of the iceberg, of course. While on that trip, I was shown pictures of container loads of pangolins, literally tens of thousands of them, headed for Vietnam or China. The pangolin accounts for something like 20% of illegal wildlife trade, all because some people believe their scales can stimulate lactation or relieve skin diseases. If a trafficker gets caught, he doesn't get significant jail time. So while wildlife crime is less lucrative than drug or human trafficking, it's less hassle and not as risky.

As long as there is a demand for body parts such as rhino horn, pangolin scales and elephant tusks in Asia, and until those African countries become richer and the poachers find a more moral way of earning good money, the devastation will continue.

I now had a good understanding of the power of television and hoped that production companies would be queuing up to make films about wildlife crime. So after making the anti-poaching film in South Africa, I was keen to get involved in a new project.

I'd worked with Grain Media's boss, an award-winning director called Orlando von Einsiedel, on the clothing brand shoot in Iceland. That Iceland gig was for a Vollebak advert I'd probably never see but it led here, to one of the most important jobs I'd do.

Orlando and Grain Media suggested I front up an investigation into the wild tiger trade. I was 100% in from the word go. We got a commission from the BBC for a film called *Tigers: Hunting the Traffickers*. That was an exciting moment. Now, instead of just shouting about it, I was going to bring this story into the living rooms of millions of people.

My producer was Jo Prichard and my director was Laura Warner, who I'd worked with on that very first TV gig in the Congo. We decided to concentrate solely on tigers because we knew lots of people had no idea about the thriving illegal trade in their body parts. Many just associated tigers with rugs but the skins are just a by-product now. Almost no part of the tiger is wasted: the bones are made into wine or glue for a variety of ailments, including arthritis, rheumatism and impotence; the flesh is eaten at extravagant banquets; the blood is drunk to strengthen the constitution; the claws and teeth are made into jewellery or used as a remedy for rabies and asthma; the whiskers are used for toothache; the tail is used to treat skin ailments; and the brain to cure laziness.

So many different agencies are involved in trying to stop this trade, including the United Nations, INTERPOL and the Convention on International Trade in Endangered Species (CITES or the Washington Convention), which more than 180 countries are signed up to. Vast numbers of tigers and thousands of tiger parts are being moved around every year, yet hardly anyone at the top of the chain seems to be held to account. As a result, the wild tiger population has plummeted from something like 100,000 tigers 100 years ago to about 4,000 today. While numbers are again on the rise in some countries, particularly India, due to anti-poaching measures and breeding programmes, there are no more than 50 tigers left in China.

In the 1980s, when most of the rest of the world agreed that killing and eating wild tigers wasn't cool (human encroachment and habitat loss are also to blame for falling tiger numbers), China and other Southeast Asian countries (most notably Thailand, Vietnam and Laos) decided to start farming them instead. Instead of sending poachers into the jungle in Malaysia, setting hundreds of snares and waiting until a tiger walked into one before smuggling the products into China and Vietnam, the criminals could produce and distribute tiger products far more easily, similar to cattle farming.

In 2007, all the countries concerned agreed to stop breeding tigers for trade. But farming, which remained in a legal grey area, didn't just continue, it boomed. There are now an estimated 8,000 tigers in farms in Southeast Asia (and probably as many in backyards in the US), about double the number left in the wild. Not only are tiger farms a welfare nightmare, but they also don't solve the problem of poaching. They complicate and undermine efforts to combat the trade in wild tiger products while legitimising the demand for tiger parts, which then puts pressure on the wild population. If you're a Chinese businessman wanting to impress some clients, you're going to want to serve wild tiger bone wine at dinner, not the cheaper farmed stuff.

My job would be to go undercover, using all of my military surveillance and reconnaissance skills to gather as much information about these farms as possible, we would ensure this evidence was passed on to the appropriate powers to help with the passing of trade sanctions or even prosecutions where possible.

We split the filming into two trips – the first to Thailand, Laos and Vietnam. In Thailand, we linked up with a courageous female wildlife crime investigator, whose name or face we couldn't reveal, who had been working for years to uncover trafficking networks. Thailand exports more captive tigers than any other country, thousands every year. Most of the tiger farms in Thailand pretend to be zoos and operate under conservation licences, which makes it difficult to get them shut down. Not that many people try, because it's not uncommon for wildlife investigators to be murdered.

At Sriracha Zoo, my investigator friend filmed hidden pens full of tigers, as far as the eye could see. That was enough for the police to raid the zoo, but they made no arrests and no tigers were removed. When we asked the zoo for comment they said allegations it was breeding tigers for illegal trade were unfair. She then received a tip-off about another zoo that had been closed to the public for two years. Laura, the director, and I gained access to Anachak Chang Zoo through a forest at its rear, before cutting through the fence. I was basically conducting a military-type Close Target Recce (CTR). This was volatile territory. Only two weeks earlier, the owner of another tiger farm had been shot dead – as is often the case with wildlife crime, he was also involved with drugs. As if that wasn't bad enough, I had no idea whether the tigers at the 'zoo' were in cages or roaming free.

There were at least 10 cats in there, some of them extremely underfed. I took photos on my phone before guard dogs got wind of my presence and started making a racket. I radioed frantically for support and after a tense few minutes, my producer Jo arrived on the scene and managed to whisk me and Laura away from danger. I'd gathered more evidence to present to the authorities and the police now do weekly checks on the zoo. The owner said the zoo was shut for renovations and was due to reopen, that his animals are well-cared for and that he has the right to keep them under a public zoo licence.

Making the tiger film wasn't as dicey as being in Colombia and Mexico tracking cartels but it was still dangerous – and Laura and I stuck out because we were clearly not local, and we had no one tracking us if anything went wrong. But the danger here was easier to rationalise. Investigations and discoveries could make a difference – if I got killed trying to give a voice to these animals, it wouldn't have been in vain.

From Thailand, live tigers are trafficked to neighbouring Laos, which is even more lawless. In Laos, the trafficking has greater ties to organised crime, while the government turns a blind eye in exchange for bribes and taxes.

A contact in Laos arranged access for us to look around Say Namthurn Zoo, where there were as many as 20 tigers, almost all of them pregnant. The contact had spotted two long chest freezers near the entrance to the zoo and asked us if we could get close enough to look inside. We took a trip there with two locals who distracted the staff while I crept away to look in the freezers. When no one was around, I sneaked a look in one of the freezers and found three frozen tiger cubs in the first and some bones and meat – clearly tiger meat – in the second.

Back at our hotel accommodation, we planned for me to return to lay camera traps to gain evidence. I completed a map study of the area to check the best route in, and discovered that the back of the facility could be accessed through about 1.6 kilometres of jungle. Laura and I were going in, so that afternoon we were dropped quickly by the minivan on the closest track to the back of the zoo. We jumped into the bushes and I navigated us through the jungle with the map and compass and by counting paces – the GPS doesn't work in a place like that. As we got closer, we could hear roaring. It was more than a little bit disconcerting to be in the thick of the jungle hearing tigers. We finally reached the perimeter of the zoo and a five-metre-high wall. Following the wall round, and working around the security camera positions, we found a gate not far from the entrance that we could climb over. I went over first to check, then came back and managed to push Laura up and over. Inside the compound, we communicated via hand signals and used jungle overgrowth to hide our movement towards the area where the freezers were. Once we were close enough, we had to find somewhere to fix the camera traps with a good view of the freezers but where they wouldn't be spotted. Then I had to test that the movement-activated cameras were working and couldn't be seen. We were lying hidden about three metres from the freezers and all the time we could hear and see people moving around close by as we steadily worked through the necessary process – just as in a military operation. I managed to set up another camera at the back of the facility looking over a suspicious waste heap, where we thought animals might be disposed of, before returning to Laura, who had remained close to the freezers. We were stuck there for an hour or so because a group of six men were talking next to the freezers and we didn't dare move. Had they seen us, I don't like to think what they would have done.

By then it was late in the afternoon, and we knew we were losing our chance to get out before it was too dark to navigate back to our collection point. Finally, we took a chance and started the hour-long trip back, before jumping from the jungle directly into the minivan as it passed slowly down the track.

When I returned to pick the camera traps up – bingo. We had captured the men removing the cubs from the freezer and loading them onto vehicles. Three weeks after that, one of the owners of the zoo was apprehended in Hanoi with seven frozen tiger cubs in the back of his car.

In Vietnam, the danger moved up another notch because the traffickers are usually armed and have direct government links. Our inside man in Nghe An was Chau Doan, a veteran investigator with contacts throughout the province. Chau went undercover to buy a block of tiger bone glue, one of the principal 'luxury' products you get from tigers. Chau described how a group of investors would pile round one of their houses and spend two or three days getting drunk while a tiger was being butchered and its bones boiled into the glue. The glue, which starts out as a pot of sticky mess, is cooled and cut into 100-gram bars which look like large stock cubes, about the size of a cigarette packet.

Killing tigers for traditional Chinese medicine wasn't a huge problem when there was only a small elite consuming it. But then, although debunked by scientists, it became seen as a status symbol, part of the culture. Products like tiger bone wine and glue don't even qualify as medicine. They're luxury goods, pure and simple. And that small elite has ballooned into a middle-class consisting of tens of millions of people, spelling disaster for the few remaining wild tigers on earth.

One tiger produces 12 bars of glue, and a kilogram of glue goes for $7,000, making it more valuable than cocaine. In Vietnam, people give glue bars as high-status presents. It's shaved into alcoholic drinks, like you might shave truffle onto a meal, to impress at a party.

Traffickers also smuggle live tiger cubs into Vietnam to be sold into the basement tiger industry. Chau posed as a trader and was driven to a property with several pens. A fat tiger can be sold for 250 million Vietnamese dong, or about $11,000, and a farm can sell seven or eight tigers a day. The tigers will then be electrocuted or drowned, before being butchered and turned into glue. Chau showed me footage of a tiger being cut up, only some of which made the finished documentary. The rest was far too gruesome.

The second part of the investigation focused on Malaysia, where we were to film with an anti-poaching team. That was a thoroughly dispiriting experience. The last time I was in that part of Malaysia was about 20 years earlier, when I was on jungle training. Then, whenever we went out on patrol, one person would have live ammunition, in case we were attacked by wild pigs (which happened) or a big cat. That's how real and prolific the threat was. We didn't actually see any tigers, but we could smell them. There was tiger scat up on a ridge line we were patrolling, and I remember waking one morning in my hammock and smelling the unmistakable scent of a large wild cat. At the age of 19, the thrill of knowing I was sharing the jungle with these animals blew my mind.

Back then, there were about 500 wild tigers in Malaysia. But that jungle I trained in has been obliterated, almost all of it turned into palm oil plantations, and tigers continue to be poached. The anti-poaching team showed us snares, which tigers step into and can't escape. If it's lucky, the poachers will return quickly and put it out of its misery. If it's not, it will die a slow and painful death. Now, there are maybe 250 tigers left at best.

From Malaysia we then flew to China. Jinjing Town in Hunan Province is home to the Sanzhen Tiger Park, which has a special permit to breed tigers for conservation purposes. The facility looked legitimate and was full of healthy-looking tigers in modern pens, but we had been tipped off that the Park may also have stores of tiger bone wine. We were watched like hawks as we moved around the park – we stood out as not just tourists, but Western tourists. The security guards tailed us as we made our way around the pens, covertly filming and making notes. But as we walked into their 'showroom', Laura and I managed to lose the guards and dart up some private stairs we had been told to check. At the top of the stairs was a cavernous room full of thousands of boxes of tiger bone wine.

At least I didn't see the production process, because that's brutal. They skin the tiger, peel off the muscles, hook the carcass through the Achilles tendon, lower it into a clay vat of cheap rice or white wine, put the lid on and leave the decomposing body to steep for up to eight years. Winemakers and sellers aren't acting illegally because they don't actually trade in tiger parts. The wine is even advertised in China – hundreds of thousands of bottles are sold each year.

That was my first real taste of investigative journalism and I found it difficult. Since leaving the military, I'd spent my whole working life keeping other people safe. If it looked like a volcano was going to blow, I'd get everyone out. If a drug trafficker wanted to kill us, I'd round everyone up and run away. But I'd gone to Asia with a big stick and poked the sleeping dragon. Wearing hidden cameras and microphones didn't sit well with me. I was happy hunting the traffickers but the low-level guys who often have no other options was more difficult to justify. But just because something makes you feel uncomfortable doesn't mean it's bad for you – it often means it's doing you some good.

I guess there's a contradiction at the heart of me. I've been trained to avoid danger at all costs, but I always seem to be running towards it. I get uncomfortable when I'm comfortable, far more so than when I'm chatting to a tiger trafficker with a wire burning into my chest and sweat pouring down my back. Where there is a danger, I grow as a person. You might say that coping with fear and pushing myself is key to who I am.

I hoped the information we'd gathered would lead to action being taken. But when Debbie Banks, from the Environmental Investigation Agency (EIA), on behalf of all the major conservation NGOs working in Southeast Asia, presented our evidence to CITES at a conference in Geneva, nothing was done. The Chinese had lobbied hard, with the result that the Laotian government was simply asked to submit a progress report in nine months' time. Debbie had seen it all before. But I was furious.

Tigers: Hunting the Traffickers was broadcast in March 2020, at about the same time as the world went into lockdown and the Netflix phenomenon *Tiger King* hit people's screens. *Tiger King*, about a bunch of big cat 'conservationists' in America, was watched by considerably more people, but I thought our film was more important.

The film led to the owner of Say Namthurn Zoo in Laos (the man found with frozen cubs in his car), being convicted and sentenced to six years for wildlife trafficking. Our positive reviews and nomination at the Grierson (British Documentary)

Awards will hopefully mean more people watching the film around the world and being more aware of the plight of tigers. The words that appear at the end of our film, though, are a depressing postscript: the Chinese government denied it was involved in the tiger trade and the Laotian government said it was committed to fighting it.

CHAPTER 14

Voyages of Discovery: Our Wondrous Planet

Remember Ittoqqortoormiit, where I headed for straight after being released from solitary confinement? Well, not only is it almost impossible to pronounce, it is also one of the most remote settlements on earth, population 345 and bathed in 24-hour daylight.

The morning after our arrival, Steve and I began our paddle up Scoresby Sound with the rest of the group, the longest fjord system in the world (the main body is about 109 kilometres long and it branches into a system of fjords covering an area of almost 15,000 square miles). And from being stuck in a black box just a day earlier, I was suddenly drenched in brilliant whiteness.

Scoresby Sound had never been paddled before in the summer, because of the extent of the sea ice. That was the reason we did it, to show how far the ice had retreated because of global warming. We were paddling in sea kayaks for about two weeks, which was hazardous in itself. If any of us had capsized, it would have been an instant emergency. Water would allow a couple of kayaks through before icing up, trapping the kayaks behind. And the ice sheets were constantly on the move, with some of them big enough to do serious damage to boats far bigger than ours. I was carrying flares and a rifle, because there was also the threat of polar bears. The ice had retreated so far north that there were now no seals or seal pups in the fjords due to the lack of solid masses of ice, which meant the bears were likely to be hungry and unpredictable.

We camped in mountaineering tents, wrapped up in multiple layers to stay warm. And because polar bears are one of the few animals that will go out of their way to hunt humans, we shared sentry duties each night, each of us doing an hour before handing over to the next person. On the third morning, we'd just finished breakfast and were packing up our kit when we saw a bear, wandering up the shingle and tundra beach towards us. We weren't worried at that point, because it must have been at least a kilometre away. The mood was more of excitement, that we'd get to see a bear so early in the trip.

However, when the bear started walking straight towards us, getting bigger and bigger with each mighty step, things got a bit tense. Our boats were too far away to run to (polar bears can reach speeds of over 25 miles per hour, which is Usain Bolt pace – and Usain Bolt never ran that fast in snow, with loads of kit on his back). The flares that were supposed to scare the bear off didn't do the trick – I might as well have released a couple of party poppers. When the bear was about 100 metres from us, it started yawning. Steve pointed out that it wasn't a sign of tiredness or boredom, but actually a sign of displacement of aggression. Then the bear started sniffing the air. It clearly found the smell of something to its liking. We had just finished breakfast, so the smell was still in the air and it was probably so hungry and desperate that it would have taken the chance at grabbing whatever was on offer.

Next, I tried firing the rifle over the bear's head, but that didn't work either. When the local driver of the kit boat fired a metre in front of the bear's feet, it finally turned and started to walk away ... before changing its mind and plodding back towards us again. In the end, we were reduced to throwing stones, shouting and banging things. It was an incredibly tense time – for many reasons. To kill the animal in self-defence was not an option. We *had* to find another way to convince it we weren't worth attacking.

Only after it had got to within about 10 metres, and been struck a few times on the feet with the small stones, did it finally give up on us. Reluctantly, it swivelled on its shovel-like paws, headed for the water and plunged in, before swimming off. To be honest, I found the experience more sad than thrilling, because if there had been enough seals around, it wouldn't have felt the need to go after us.

Having reached the northern edge of the sea ice after about 10 days, the plan was to climb previously unexplored mountains in the Stauning Alps. But to reach the unexplored mountains, we had to ski for a couple of days pulling pulks (sledges with our kit in) and wade across rivers of freezing meltwater to reach the glacier. That involved removing our trousers, socks and shoes so that none of our kit got wet, and trying not to get swallowed up by quicksand. In case you were wondering, Greenland rivers aren't warm, and my testicles ended up somewhere near my Adam's apple.

Most of the routes we wanted to climb had avalanched, making the snowpack too dangerous. (Two expert mountaineers, Tamsin Gay and Libby Peter, were tasked with the recceing). But we eventually made our way up, becoming the first people to do so. Steve reached the top first, which meant he got to name the mountain. Because his wife was due to give birth six weeks later, it's now known as Mount Usiliac, which is Inuit for 'firstborn son'.

★   ★   ★

Our next port of call for the series was Oman, which is one of the most jaw-droppingly stunning countries I've ever visited. Northeast Oman is among the driest places on earth but shaped by water, which has carved deep canyons, or wadis, into the landscape. Our goal was to abseil into a previously unexplored (or, as we called it, 'un-dropped') canyon in the Al-Hajar mountain range, but first we had to get in some training.

Working with a guy called Justin Halls, who lives in Oman, our first job was to rig the second largest cave chamber in the world, called Majlis al Jinn (Cave of the Genie), so that Steve and a cameraman could abseil into it for the documentary's opening sequence. There was nothing particularly complicated about it, but because we were rigging for two days in 40-degree heat, it took a lot out of me, without me really noticing.

Next up was a 'training' abseil off Jebel Shams, Oman's highest mountain. Jebel Shams has canyons a kilometre deep, and the one that had been chosen for the dress rehearsal represented one of the longest single-drop abseils on the planet and had only been explored once before by Khaled Abdul Malak, a Lebanese dentist who had made exploring these canyons his life's work. He was also our guide on this expedition. This canyon dropped 400 metres, which is four times the height of Big Ben. (The longest commercial operated singe-drop abseil is 204 metres, down the Maletsunyane waterfall in Lesotho, while the most I had ever abseiled in a single drop before was 200 metres.) This was a bit like going 12 rounds with Tyson Fury to tune up for a fight with Anthony Joshua a few days later.

It was a trek just to get to the top of the canyon, involving donkeys (which I'm allergic to) and searing heat. The range is 2,000 metres above sea level and was once seabed, so there were fossils of shells everywhere we looked. We camped overnight in an abandoned village (lack of water has become a big problem in Oman, which is why abandoned settlements pepper the landscape), before Justin and I rose at first light and got to work rigging the top section of the exposed rockface. The following day, we spent eight hours rigging two sets of rope, both 400 metres long (we'd had them specially made, because a normal rope is only half that length).

When we were finally done, by about 3pm, I was totally fried from drilling holes and installing ropes with the sun behind me and reflecting off the wall. There was also the stress of being that high up, which burns through energy. I was drinking litres of water, but it wasn't making much difference. Ironically, I'd done a piece to camera on the trek there about the dangers of heat exhaustion. And now I was beginning to suffer from exactly that.

We collectively decided it would be too dangerous for the crew to attempt, so they would stay the night at the top before driving off the mountain and meeting up with us in a day or two at the other end of the canyon. I don't blame them, because I was absolutely gripped. If you watch the documentary, you can see the fear in my eyes. But Steve being Steve, he was keen to crack on that night, with the abseiling team filming on helmet cams.

It was now the hottest part of the day, over 40°C. Not ideal conditions for a 400-metre abseil. I should have told Steve I wasn't feeling great and to wait until the morning, but I didn't. I don't know why. When I watched the film back later, I was struck by how vacant my eyes were and how hoarse my voice was. I was obviously dehydrated, and presumably I wasn't thinking straight.

Steve went first and made it to the bottom in about 25 minutes, with no problems. Then it was my turn. When I got on

217

the ropes, my tongue felt like a strip of leather that had cracked right down the middle and was glued to the roof of my mouth, as if by a Pritt Stick. Because the drop was so long, we decided to use a caving rack descender, a variable friction device to dissipate the heat. There aren't many commercial descenders that would have taken the battering of a straight 400-metre drop. But almost as soon as I started my descent, I realised I hadn't put enough friction through my device. I pulled the brake, before hauling up the rope from underneath and feeding it through the descender. That's when I realised exactly how buggered I was.

It took me about 10 minutes to pull up this section of rope, after which I was in pieces (400 metres of rope weighs about 40 kilograms, plus I had a 30-kilogram bag hanging between my legs). I'd still only dropped about 20 metres from the ledge and was hanging in the air 380 metres from the bottom, with a heavy bag of kit, cramping up and barely able to see straight. Shame I couldn't take in the view, because it's one of the most beautiful on the planet.

I started to lower myself down again, but now I'd given myself too much friction. I should have put the extra friction through my harness, or the karabiner on my harness, and let gravity do the work. Instead, every time I dropped 15 centimetres, I was having to drag up 30 centimetres more rope to feed through the descender. The sun was starting to set, my only way out of the canyon was down, and I was pretty much a broken man. Not a situation anyone wants to find themselves in. I kept thinking, 'I'm the rope rescue guy, and I'm stuck. No one still up top has the skills to get me out of here.'

I inched my way down for about an hour (when it should have taken about 15 minutes) until I was about 100 metres from the bottom, by which time I couldn't even grip the rope and sweat was literally pouring from my helmet. I was tipping it out, as if it was a bucket. My fingers were curled inwards, like talons, and my whole body had seized up. On the documentary, it looks like I'm about to nod off on the rope. It was getting dark, and Steve must have been wondering what the hell I was up to. Eventually, I was able to yell down to Steve to grab the bottom of the rope and lower me down the last 50 metres, fireman's belay style.

When I finally reached the bottom, an hour after beginning my descent, I was really pissed off with myself. I should have put my foot down and said to Steve, 'I know you're feeling fresh and want to get this done, but I'm not feeling too great. Me and Justin have been rigging almost non-stop since we arrived and haven't eaten all day. Let's wait until we're properly rested.' That would have been the safe and sensible thing to do.

I was also angry at performing such a horrible abseil on film. It wasn't much consolation that Justin's descent was as ragged as mine. Like me, the poor bloke got cramp and couldn't hold on to the rope properly. For ages, we could only see the speck of his headlamp. After lowering him down the final section, we didn't even set up camp. Our crazy Lebanese canyon explorer guide, Khaled Abdul Malak, whooped all the way down on his turn. And after guzzling litres of water laced with electrolytes, we crawled inside our sleeping bags, put up our mosquito nets and zonked out under a rock.

Expeditions always ask that you go the extra mile. Like my mate Waldo Etherington, who does pretty much the same job I do, often says: 'If it was easy, it wouldn't be hard'. They are gruelling and, in a lot of cases, quite high stakes with minimal returns. It's often hard to convey just how dangerous some situations actually are, and in this industry you don't get a second chance. The juxtaposition is that a death or serious injury is inexcusable and would put the kybosh on the entire world of adventure TV (for a while at least), but the adventure and perceived risk are all part of that. It's a fine balance we all walk daily and have to adhere to, even when editorial and environmental circumstances push us in other directions.

I'd begun to think I was the only person who'd got himself into a pickle on Steve's expeditions (remember, I'd also snapped my ankle ligaments in West Papua) because of the amount of grafting I was doing. Steve once said to me jokingly, 'You're the only one who seems to get injured.' And I was happy with that as it meant nobody else was. I had a lot resting on my shoulders, trying to keep things running smoothly and everybody safe. It played on my mind a lot. That no one else had been injured or unwell was testament to the amount of planning and safety procedures in place, with support by True to Nature and Secret Compass.

I was wearing lots of different hats – head of safety, head of security, medic, rigger, appearing on camera and sorting out logistics. After a hard day's trekking, I'd be preparing dinner. After the crew went to bed, I'd be sorting out kit and chatting with the producer about the following day's schedule. All the while, I'd be trying to keep the morale bubbling nicely. It all stems from the Commando Spirit: courage, determination, unselfishness and cheerfulness in the face of adversity.

That Commando Spirit was why I kept getting invited back by programme makers. But because I used to be a Marine, people seemed to think that nothing bad could happen to me. It's true that I was a safe pair of hands and 99% of the time I had everything under control. But having an insatiable appetite for hard work, and always wanting to be tested, can catch up with you. I was spreading myself too thin, which is why I sometimes came apart.

Oscar Wilde said that 'experience is the hardest kind of teacher', because it gives you the test first and the lesson afterwards. But the lessons you learn from flunking tests can be the most valuable. With plenty more of Steve's expeditions to go, that was a useful thing to bear in mind. But it also works the other way. In the military, the first thing you do after any operation is have a hot debrief. Even if the operation had the desired result, you never conclude that everything went well. You always ask what could have been done better. I do the same in everyday life. If you don't ask questions of yourself when things go wrong, you'll keep making the same mistakes. And if you don't ask questions of yourself when things go right, you'll never get better.

After waking up under a rock, the four of us – me, Steve, Justin and Khaled – spent the next two days making our way out of the canyon. That trek included another 700 metres of descent, and we were carrying the equivalent of fridges on our backs. I was still a bit sore, but back to something like normal after guzzling litres of water. I spent the next two days at the hotel, shaking out and repacking the kit, before we headed off to the final destination of the expedition, the canyon system that had never been explored before.

The descent from our drop-off point was something like 1,200 metres, and the canyon system was 5,000 metres long. But that's all that was known about it. We didn't know how big each of the drops was, or whether it would be feasible for the film crew and their kit to complete the route. Water was also going to be a problem. Each member of the team would need to drink about a litre an hour, to stave off dehydration and heat exhaustion, but there was only a certain amount we could carry. That being the case, we'd need to discover water on the way. If we didn't, we'd be in serious trouble.

We set off at 6am, to cover as much ground as possible before the sun got roasting. After several hours and abseils, things were getting a bit dicey on the water front, until Khaled came across a stagnant pond. If you filtered the water – and avoided the scorpions – it was fine to drink. Then we found what we'd been looking for, a sheer drop of about 80 metres, straight into an inviting looking pool below.

We spent the night at the top before abseiling down in the morning. This time, we managed to get all the crew to the bottom. The pool was teeming with life – frogs, butterflies, giant dragonflies – and fringed with pink flowers. It was the perfect metaphor for why I do what I do: getting to that pool hadn't been easy, had involved blood, sweat and very nearly tears, but this was the reward, a little bit of paradise that no one had ever seen before. To be able to share that experience with our little gang was just a beautiful feeling. Often on expeditions it's the people who make the mission memorable and worthwhile – the bond of friendship that's forged in war or expedition is often the strongest, it's that camaraderie that counters the extreme hardship.

But it wasn't long before reality set in. Clouds started gathering and scuttling overhead, suggesting rain was imminent. If we were caught in a flash flood, we would all be dead. This was nature saying, 'Yes, I can be beautiful, but don't get complacent.' Then, as if nature wanted to hammer home the point, just below the pool we saw a couple of saw-scaled vipers, which are one of the most lethal species of snake on the planet. After doing a piece to camera about how incredibly dangerous they are, Steve picked one of them up with a stick. I've watched Steve handle some of the most venomous animals on the planet and I'm always blown away by his instantaneous encyclopaedic descriptions, while dancing round flashing fangs or teeth to get the perfect shot.

Then it started raining, just as we were entering a particularly tight section of canyon that could have turned into a raging torrent in a matter of minutes. That was a tense hour or so, with not much talking. Luckily, we just made it out in time, before reaching the water of the valley of Wadi al Hijri, with its crystal-clear pools, streams and waterfalls. We'd reached the end of the unexplored canyon. Or what was an unexplored canyon, before we turned up.

After that Oman expedition, I was quite chuffed with how things were panning out. Steve and I had built a good dynamic, like the camaraderie you have between a superhero and a side-kick. Our on-screen relationship was a constant thread, holding things together, and I could tell it would work well when the editors did their thing.

I had two weeks off after Oman (luxury!) before heading out to Suriname. Suriname is a small country on the north-east coast of South America, surrounded by Guyana to the west, French Guiana to the east and Brazil to the south. It has a population of about half a million and is covered in pristine rainforest. At first sight, almost everything about the country seems untouched by modernisation. Its international airport is in the middle of the jungle and you can fly for hours without seeing anything but trees.

Suriname's capital Paramaribo, located on the banks of the Suriname River, is an amazing melting pot of a city. The old part is a UNESCO World Heritage Site, a Dutch colonial town almost unchanged since the eighteenth century. Its population is a mash-up of people whose ancestors came from the Indian subcontinent, sub-Saharan Africa and Java, along with smaller groups, such as Creole-Mulatto, indigenous Indians (Amerindians) and Europeans.

Those of African descent, called Maroons and whose ancestors were taken to Suriname to work as slaves, have retained a lot of the ancient traditions. The first time I visited a Maroon village, I was dumbfounded. There were women smashing up cassava leaves to make fufu, a staple I'd seen people making in several West African countries. The village was dotted with long huts and everyone was speaking a West African dialect. I could have been in central Democratic Republic of the Congo. But because the Maroons are so remote and relatively untouched, anthropologists study them to understand how people would have lived in West Africa a few hundred years ago, before ships started taking slaves across the Atlantic.

The plan was to spend five weeks in Suriname, exploring tepuis and two unnamed river courses that no Europeans had been down before. Our first objective had no name and we affectionately named it Ghost River or YiYi, as it wasn't on any maps. By now, I'd learned to be careful with my words on camera. I'd never stand on top of a mountain and say, 'We are the first people to be here.' If we were, so be it. But I didn't know that for a fact. In some cases, indigenous people would have been aware of our 'discoveries' thousands of years ago. So instead, I'd think, '*I've* never been here before, so it's new to *me*.' That's a good attitude to have in everyday life. Sometimes when I'm driving in the UK, I'll say to Anna, 'Let's take a different route, we might see something new.' That way, what might have been a mundane journey becomes a voyage of discovery.

While we weren't always the first, I guarantee that no one in TV has immersed themselves so fully in their work as Steve and

I did during the course of those expeditions. Everything you see on TV is condensed, and some viewers probably think we spend most of our time in hotels. But we spent 34 days in Suriname, sleeping out almost every night (over the course of the 11 months and 10 expeditions, we slept out over a hundred nights, probably way more, sometimes in tents, sometimes in hammocks, sometimes under rocks). We became part of nature, rather than voyeurs, which is why we were doing something special.

Having been flown deep into the jungle by plane – the landing strip was grass, the few buildings were long since deserted – we were then lifted even further into the interior by helicopter. After that we completed a couple of days' paddling and there was a classic example of the ancients knocking us down a peg or two. The course had been very narrow, which meant having to drag our inflatable canoes under and over countless tangles of fallen branches. This was uncharted territory, not on any maps, so we were doing the usual and congratulating each other about being the first people to see what we were seeing. Then I came across some strange marks on the rocks. I asked one of our guides what they were, and he told me they were made by ancient hunter-gatherers, from sharpening axes and arrowheads around 500 to 1,000 years ago.

In the middle of the jungle, nothing had really changed for millions of years. It was teeming with wildlife. We saw giant river otters, caimans, spider and howler monkeys and gibbons. A tapir, the largest wild animal in South America, waded out right in front of us. It didn't know to be afraid of humans, because it had never seen any. We didn't see any jaguars, but we did discover some jaguar droppings. One day, an almost-legendary harpy eagle swooped down and landed on a branch above us. I'd put a hook in the water and pull out a wolf fish or giant piranha

225

in seconds (the piranha, the biggest in the world, had teeth the size of a small dog's). We'd have one for dinner and smoke another overnight for breakfast. There were also stingrays, which can do serious damage if you step on them.

But forget about killer stingrays, the really bad news is that some of those wolf fish and piranhas are now being exported to China, where they go for thousands of dollars, to live out the rest of their days in aquariums. Gold mining companies have also got their talons into Suriname. We filmed a gold mine, which was a lot bigger than we expected.

Everywhere we visited for that series, the local people said that the last five years have been more out of kilter than they could ever remember. The rains weren't coming, or there was too much. Water levels were too low, the ice had retreated, forests weren't just being thinned out, they were disappearing. Diseases were popping up all over the place, often caused by interactions between people and wildlife that didn't happen before. Previously pristine environments had become Petri dishes, with viruses jumping between wild animals and humans (scientists believe SARS and MERS came from bats, via domesticated animals, and it's likely that coronavirus originated in live animal markets in China, although that hasn't been confirmed at the time of writing).

In Suriname, people told us that they were having to go further and further upstream to find wolf fish, because so many were being sold to the Chinese. At least Suriname has anti-logging measures in place, which means it remains stunningly beautiful. But anti-anything measures often only last until a company makes an offer the government can't refuse.

You can be philosophical about the human destruction of the planet. Earth is 4.5 billion years old, while humans have only been wrecking things for the last 12–15,000 years (the so-called

'Agricultural Revolution'). That's such a small speck of time and suggests the planet will simply move on once we've passed through. But what humans are doing to the planet now is simply unsustainable. Yes, humans have been migrating across the planet for tens of thousands of years. But for much of that time, their numbers were small and their technology basic, meaning there was only so much damage they could do. The population explosion combined with technological advances has changed the game completely. Most of the world's deforestation and devastation of wildlife and natural resources has happened in the last 100 years. It's not about the planet moving on after we've gone, it's about us destroying the planet while we're still here. We are now entering the Anthropocene, the age where human impact is forever bound to the earth – and anyone with kids should be terrified by that.

Exploring the world has provided me with some incredible experiences, but it also means I've seen the worst of humanity. And here's an irony: travelling to these remote places has taught me how fragile the world is and turned me into a conservationist, but it's also taught me that I'm part of the problem. The more time I spend exploring, the more time I spend on planes. And by going to these places and making television programmes about them, I'm encouraging others to follow in my footsteps. People are probably reading this and thinking, 'Suriname sounds great, I'd like to go there.' Modern explorers have very modern dilemmas.

That said, Steve's *Expedition* series was the first carbon-neutral project UKTV had ever produced. Plus it had an environmental education slant. Steve didn't think it was enough to show viewers how wonderful the natural world was, he thought we should also be showing the damage we were doing. Because of people like Steve, at least we know the extent of the damage being done. Persuading governments to do something about it is another thing entirely, but it starts with seeing and discussing the problems and starting the paradigm shift.

For days in the Suriname jungle, we were looking at the map and thinking there must be rapids coming up – the contours were getting tighter and we had a lot of altitude to drop before sea level. Then one evening, when we stopped paddling to set up our hammocks, we heard a rumbling. We followed our ears and found a full-on cataract (a cataract being a section of continual waterfalls) that was 100 metres long and almost as high. If Indian tribes had ever been aware of the waterfall, they'd stopped telling people about it at some point, because it wasn't on any map or known locally.

It later transpired that we'd stumbled upon one of the largest waterfalls in Suriname, which is not something that happens every day. Our guide Ila was moved to tears by the sheer beauty of it, and the fact that there were still such glorious treasures to find in his country. He had the honour of naming it and plumped for 'Gang gan jin di wan', meaning 'The Biggest One'. We affectionately nicknamed it Ila Falls.

We spent all day and another night at the waterfall, simply because it was too beautiful to leave, before paddling all the way out to join another big river system. Then, after resting up for a few days in a village called Amatopo (whose inhabitants call themselves 'wasp people'), a helicopter flew us up to the top of Tafelberg tepui, which has been cut off from the rainforest below for millions of years and is a haven for endemic species.

We camped right on the edge of a crystal-clear river, which ran straight over the side of the tepui. And when morning came,

Steve, Graham the cameraman and I abseiled down into a gully that opened out into a deep pool. What we found below was like a lost world. There were hummingbirds and different kinds of wolf fish, and Steve was particularly taken by giant damselflies and poison dart frogs. He even found a giant, venomous centipede in his shoe, which only Steve could think was a bonus. Working with Steve, I learned early on the difference between 'poisonous' and 'venomous'. I asked Steve once if a certain snake was poisonous. He said, 'No, it's venomous. There is only one snake which is both poisonous and venomous.' A venomous animal projects or bites its victims to protect itself while a poisonous animal uses passive mechanisms to secrete its poison, such as if another animal touches or eats it.

The plan was to abseil down a waterfall into a gorge system and try to follow the river course down all the way to the forest below, but running out of rope and almost getting killed – again! – put paid to that. We'd just taken refuge under an overhang, which was to be our bedroom for the night, when we heard a massive 'whoof', followed by an explosion. A boulder roughly the size of a microwave oven had hit the deck where I'd just been standing. Had it landed seconds earlier, it would have turned me into pink mist.

As it turned out, I got out of Suriname with just a broken thumb.

In Bhutan, we paddled down the tiny Himalayan kingdom's last unrun river, the terrifying Chamkar Chhu. No one had attempted to paddle down it before because it ran through the country's steepest gorge and local legend said it fell off the edge of the planet. Steve assembled a crack team, including a freestyle world champion, a big drop specialist and a Himalayan veteran.

But not even a blessing from some local monks, who asked the river spirits to watch over us, assuaged our fears.

The expedition began in the town of Bumthang, just south of Gangkhar Puensum, the highest unclimbed mountain in the world (one for the bucket list). The gorge runs for 40 kilometres, but the team had no idea how far they'd get. Satellite images showed that there was only one obvious evacuation point and that the support rafts, carrying camping kit, medical supplies, food and thousands of pounds of equipment, wouldn't make the first section. That meant I'd be tracking their progress on foot and any filming would have to be done on helmet cameras.

The tighter the river got, the angrier it got, which I found terrifying to watch. When stuff goes wrong in white water, it goes horribly wrong. Because white water moves so fast, everything comes apart very quickly, which makes managing safety extremely difficult. Sure enough, on day one, Steve almost came a cropper. The team had just passed a point where two rivers combined, doubling the volume of water – when Steve dropped off a boulder and into a 'stopper'.

Stoppers occur when water is driven up over a rock and then downwards, creating a tumble dryer effect. Steve was immediately dragged under and spun over and over, and it was only the quick thinking of big drop specialist Sal Montgomery, who clambered onto a rock, threw Steve a rope and managed to drag him out, that saved the day. I'd been through some pretty hairy situations with Steve, but this was the closest shave he'd had with death. And that's why it made for such compelling TV.

I actually had a couple of months off before Steve's second expedition in Oman, which was a trip to the remote Jebel Samhan mountain range in the south of the country. Oman has one of the world's fastest-growing populations, which means wildlife is being pushed into smaller and smaller pockets. Jebel Samhan is one such sanctuary, home to some of the last remaining Arabian leopards on earth. Our main mission was to complete the first ascent of a previously unexplored cliff face. If we found any signs of Arabian leopards, great. If we saw one, I might have considered retirement.

The section Steve had chosen was roughly 600 metres high and almost perpendicular. Thousands of years of weathering had created hollows and caves, which meant we could attack it over a few days, setting up camp and sleeping on ledges. As ever, Steve had invited along a couple of legends, Hazel Findlay and John Arran, two of the best climbers in the world. Their job would be to find a route up, before Steve came up behind them and I started hoisting all the kit up, along with my old mate Justin Halls. And we had a lot of kit, hundreds of kilograms of it. Climbing kit, rigging kit, camera kit, plus food and over 100 litres of water.

We found leopard scat in the foothills, so knew they were around somewhere. Our companion Khaled had spent more than 10 years studying the leopard population in the region and placed remote cameras across the mountain range a month before our arrival. With any luck, our prize for reaching the top of the escarpment would be leopards caught on film.

Even Hazel and John seemed intimidated when we reached the bottom of the cliff. And when Hazel started making her way up, she soon discovered that the rock had the consistency of cheese. The cliff was actually limestone and once would have been at the bottom of the sea, which was now a few miles away. A sedimentary rock, limestone is composed almost entirely of fossils, the remains of ancient plants and animals. On a more practical level, it has a habit of breaking off in your fingers. But as long as it had the consistency of cheddar and not stilton, we weren't backing down.

Having spent hours hoisting kit to the first pitch, we got our heads down for the night. When we awoke the following morning, we were shrouded in mist, which had rolled in from the sea. This was a classic expedition situation: 12 hours earlier, we'd been frying in the sun. Now we were going to have to climb half-blind in the freezing cold. And the higher we climbed, the more cheese-like the rock became.

But as I've already noted, the harder expeditions are, the sweeter the rewards. On the second night, having made our camp in a deep gash about 200 metres up, we discovered the fossilised skeleton of a whale. After dying, it had sunk to the bottom of the sea and become covered in a layer of smaller organisms, which had then been washed away. That blew my mind. No one had ever been on that cliff face – that I can safely say – so we were the first people to lay eyes on that whale, which had to be tens of millions of years old.

When we finally made it to the top the following day, Khaled was there to greet us with his laptop. Crowded around the screen, we watched film of foxes, honey badgers, partridges and ibex. That sea mist sustains plant life, which those animals can feed on. It all makes perfect sense. And then we hit the mother lode: two Arabian leopards, a female and a male in hot pursuit, showing signs that he was about to mate. Khaled had almost 40 clips, crucial for his conservation work. But watching those clips was also quite sobering: only in those mountains did those leopards feel safe, and only because humans couldn't reach them.

To be honest, I wasn't really looking forward to the final expedition in Borneo. I'd first visited the island in 1997, when I did my initial jungle training in the Malaysian section, and knew there had been a shocking amount of deforestation since then. The thought of witnessing the destruction of such an important ecosystem depressed me, and the actual expedition didn't thrill me much either. The plan was to search for undocumented cave art in the Indonesian jungle. If we did find any in this remote location, then maybe it would also become part of the proposed UNESCO World Heritage Site, meaning the area would be protected from logging, quarrying and the expansion of oil palm plantations, at least in theory. I kept thinking, 'This is going to be dull. I don't want to hack through jungle for days to see some handprints. I've already seen them in Mexico. Where's the action? Where's the adventure?' Looking back, I'd been spoilt.

The caves are situated in the Sangkulirang-Mangkalihat Karst, one of the last remaining areas of intact jungle in Borneo and formed by the dissolution of rocks such as limestone and gypsum. Karst (limestone peaks) covered in jungle is one of the hardest environments to operate in. Limestone erodes quite easily, which means the jungle floor in Borneo is pockmarked with sinkholes and cave openings, hidden beneath the plant life (despite the dangers, our guides opted for flip-flops). There are also sharp limestone spikes, or blades, that rise up from the earth and cut through the canopy.

Paddling into the jungle on longboats, I was quite encouraged by the density of the foliage which, combined with the treach-erous limestone, suggested it was difficult for loggers, quarrymen and farmers to penetrate. On several occasions, our path was blocked by fallen trees, which we had to cut up with a chainsaw. Not ideal in a crocodile infested river. But Dr Pindi Setiawan, the local archaeologist who was part of our team, assured me that Chinese companies were determined and wealthy enough to reach parts of Borneo that companies from other countries couldn't. If these Chinese companies had their way, they'd chop down every tree on the island and grind all the limestone into dust, to make cement to help build their ever-expanding cities.

After a few days, the river started to become shallow and we eventually reached a point where our boats couldn't penetrate any further. We spent the next two days setting up a base camp and sorting out logistics. I still wasn't that excited about the cave paintings, until I got chatting to Pindi around the fire. Pindi explained that not much archaeology had been done in the region, for the same reason that not much logging, quarrying or farming had been done, because it was simply so remote and too hard to navigate. As such, until recently cave art was thought to have developed in Europe during the last ice age. But archaeologists now believe it was being created much earlier in Borneo, when it wasn't an island but formed the easternmost tip of the vast continental region of Eurasia. When Pindi told me that some of the recently discovered cave paintings were at least 40,000 years old, I started to get excited.

Our guides were bird's nest collectors, like the guys I'd worked with in the Malaysian part of the island. Nowadays, collectors in the Sangkulirang-Mangkalihat Karst build nesting towers for the swifts, which means they don't have to trek for weeks to reach caves in the middle of the jungle. But they remembered the area from when they were kids, accompanying their fathers on collecting trips, and in 2018 guided Pindi to a spectacular cave, containing possibly the oldest figurative art in the world.

The huge cave was situated on top of a mountain ridge and was home to some of the most beautiful paintings I'd ever seen, from any period. This stuff made the rock art I'd seen in Mexico almost modern, closer in age to Damien Hirst than the Palaeolithic. On one wall was a huge painting of a wild bull, or banteng. On another wall, about seven-and-a-half metres off the ground, were roughly 20 human handprints, which I could just about reach by clambering up onto a little ledge. The handprints were stencils, in that the artist created them by placing a hand on the rock (usually the left one) and spraying paint over it with a blow pipe, which was held in their right hand. It boggled my mind that I was standing exactly where those ancient people stood and seeing exactly what they saw from a time where Borneo wasn't a jungle. (The jungle only appeared about 8,000 years ago, hence the savannah animal paintings.)

When I hovered my hands over their prints, a chill went up my spine, because it felt like I was sharing a special moment with someone from the mists of time. From feeling under-whelmed at the beginning of the expedition, it suddenly felt like the most worthwhile expedition I'd ever been on.

We ventured further into the jungle, hoping to find more. The first couple of days, we schlepped for miles and climbed for hours to reach a cave, only to find nothing inside. But then our luck changed. One morning, we came upon a small opening. Steve and I got on our hands and knees, slithered past a huge beehive and switched on our head torches. Above us were more ancient handprints, tens of thousands of years old. Not even the bird's nest collectors had seen these messages, coloured pink and dark red and speckled with dots. I also discovered an etching of a deer, and apertures like portholes on a ship through which the people who made these handprints would have looked out on the vastness below.

It struck me as incredible that people living thousands of years ago and thousands of miles apart were creating almost identical art. What better proof that everyone on earth is wired the same. Wherever I travel in the world, I'm always amazed by how similar people are, from Inuit in the Arctic to remote tribes in the Papuan jungle. They need the same basics such as food, water and shelter, but they also need to express the feelings in their heads, in the form of art and culture. And the more you think about how similar everyone is, wherever they live in the world, whatever colour they are or whatever their beliefs, the stranger it seems that people are constantly fighting about their perceived differences.

If Pindi and others could persuade UNESCO the cave art was important enough – and not only the cave art, but also the incredible flora and fauna, including blind fish, rare bats, insects, crabs, spiders and orangutans, as well as the indigenous Lebbo' people who incorporate cave paintings in their narratives – then maybe that jungle could be saved.

Of all the Steve Backshall expeditions I've been on, that was the least action-packed and gung-ho. Yes, it was knackering, involving day after day of yomping through the densest jungle and living hand to mouth, and there was none of the sexy stuff, like abseiling or white-water rafting. However, that trip to Borneo made me rethink. Sometimes, you don't need all that sexy Action Man stuff. Discovering that cave art was one of my most profound moments, and among the most important things I've ever done.

CHAPTER 15

No Better Way to Live: You Have One Life

I'm writing this as I hold my four-week-old son. And did I mention I married Anna? We managed to fit in the wedding in Glencoe a week after I returned from Southeast Asia and two weeks after she came home from the Serengeti.

Since getting into a relationship in 2016, we'd spent more time apart than we had together. When I wasn't off on my adventures, Anna was on hers. Sometimes, we wouldn't even speak for weeks because we were both working tough and stressful 18-hour days in the middle of nowhere. We literally didn't have time to call home, but Anna gets it. I *have* to do what I do, and so does she.

Back in January 2020, I was on a National Geographic production called *Welcome to Earth* in Namibia, rigging Harasib cave in the Dragon's Breath complex, home to the world's largest non-glacial underground lake, ahead of the actual shoot with the Hollywood star Will Smith scheduled for a few months later. A few weeks after that, I flew to South Sudan, for a BBC documentary about the functionally extinct northern white rhino, which people haven't given up hope of finding in the wild.

Towards the end of the trip, Anna was telling me about a pandemic that was sweeping across the world. When she suggested we might have to pack up and come home early because they were talking about locking the UK down, I thought she was being dramatic. But sure enough, on 16 March we got a satellite call from the BBC's Natural History Unit in Bristol, telling us to return immediately.

We collapsed our bush camp, packed our kit, loaded everything onto the helicopters and returned to the capital Juba. From Juba, we flew back to London via Addis Ababa, and straight into a national lockdown. My life had suddenly screeched to a halt.

From a situation where Anna and I were snatching a day together here and there, we were now living together for weeks on end. And you know what? That worked as well. We'd just moved from London to a flat in Bristol, right on the Downs, and it was lovely getting to know Bristol properly. We went for long walks and wild swims. We caught up on all the things we'd done over the past year and discussed the future.

When the rules relaxed, Foxy and I did some exploring around Bristol. I drew up a programme of caving, climbing and free-diving, to name but a few. We even went out with the RNLI on the River Severn.

Anna and I had both spent so much time abroad, working in exotic locations, that we'd become blasé about the wonders on our own doorstep. Just getting outside is therapy. Feeling the wind, rain and sun on your face is therapy. Listening to the birds is therapy. Smelling wet grass is therapy. If you're feeling brave, find some fresh water and take a dip. Embrace the discomfort, learn to love the sound of your teeth chattering. In difficult times, nature has this amazing ability to freshen up the mind and clear it of clutter and negativity.

Instagram has created a generation that wants to be fit on a cosmetic level. When people see me on the cover of *Men's Health* magazine, they assume I'm a massive gym bunny. But that's not true. Lifting and shifting kit and my own bodyweight around is hard work.

Mostly I'm in good shape as a by-product of my job, and learning and practising the skills I need to do it. I spend weeks and months up a mountain or in the jungle without a gym or equipment.

During lockdown, I came up with Expedition Fit, a fitness programme that's a mixture of callisthenics, lifting, compound exercises and running. Physical and mental fitness go hand in hand, and being stuck at home wasn't going to stop me prioritising my physical health. I know that if I'm physically fit, I'll be mentally strong and productive. '*Mens sana in corpore sano*' – healthy mind in a healthy body. Exercise is my religion. Making physical fitness a priority helps with my mental fitness, making the mind more agile and open to new ideas and opportunities.

I definitely have a positive attitude, and my training and experience have bolstered that. Many times I've been close to death, and my time in Iraq was key to me taking control of my life choices. Witnessing the Ebola outbreak in Africa also had a major effect on me. You can't see that much death and suffering and be the same again. It taught me that life is fragile, so I needed to do as much as I could with it. The feeling when I was released from the nuclear bunker and saw the rolling countryside and the beautiful blue sky afresh, or the sight of an ancient handprint made in a time I can barely imagine – they are all reminders that our lives are precious. We have a limited amount of time on this planet. It was Confucius who said, 'We have two lives. The second begins when we realise we only have one.' (These philosophers know a thing or two.)

Often, someone will tell me how lucky I am, being able to do what I do. But it has very little to do with luck. Mostly, good luck is when opportunity and preparation meet. I've put in a huge amount of hard work and training and time to be able to earn a living by adventure. I had to graft like crazy for a couple of decades, get qualifications, make sacrifices and deal with rejection. When you have a worthy goal in mind, success is almost guaranteed – but only if you put the hard yards in, over an extended period of time. There's nothing magic about it. I didn't become a sniper in the Royal Marines overnight, it took me years to get there, going right back to when I was hiking every weekend and learning to tie knots in the Scouts. I wasn't exceptional, some kind of whizz kid, I just worked hard and stuck the course. Even in the Marines, I wasn't better at things than other people. In fact, I was pretty average. I just always wanted to better myself, which hasn't changed. It's the same in any world, from business to sport. The kids who make it as Premier League footballers aren't always the most talented, they're often 'just' the hardest grafters. Some with more talent don't make it, because they expect things to come easily and don't put in the necessary work.

When I give talks to kids, the first thing I tell them is: 'I'm living proof that you can have almost anything you want – if you want it hard enough.' We are masters of our own destinies. I show them pictures of stuff I've done: me in a volcano in the Congo, me rowing across the Atlantic to break a world record for charity, me being chased by a rhino. I don't really have to say much because kids have boundless imaginations that are easily sparked. I wish someone had told me when I was younger that I could do this stuff – for a job. I wish someone had said, 'You become what you think about.'

I have to be honest, 2020 worked out okay for me, despite all the bad stuff that was going on in the world. As well as various trips abroad, I signed up for a groundbreaking new project – a deep ocean exploration/conservation series for National Geographic. *Mission OceanXplorers* will follow a state-of-the-art ocean research vessel, *Ocean Xplorer*, owned by American billionaire philanthropist Ray Dalio. The BBC's *Blue Planet* team are also involved, as is James Cameron, who directed *Titanic* and *Avatar*.

In theory, I'm the guy who's running it all – Mission Ops. And by the time you read this, it should be in the can. Being leagues under the sea is uncharted territory for me, as it is for almost everyone on the planet. And the fact that 95% of the oceans are unexplored means I'm sure we'll find something new.

The other major project has been our lockdown baby. I naturally thought I'd have to miss out on *Mission OceanXplorers* when we found out that Anna was pregnant. After discussing the situation at length, though, we decided it was too big an opportunity to miss. So when Atlas was born, I was watching on WhatsApp from the *OceanXplorer* vessel in the Caribbean, having spent the morning diving with a pod of humpback whales. It's that sacrifice again that I spoke about.

We talked through the options together and Anna and I saw the bigger picture. We knew that after filming, I'd be at home for a couple of months. And I wouldn't just see the baby for an hour or so every evening, like most working dads, I'd be able to be with him 24 hours a day. I wanted to be there for our baby's life, not just the birth. We were confident we'd make it work.

Family is very important to me. I try to speak to my siblings – my twin Ross, a Marine for 16 years; my sister Stroma, who is living a far quieter life than me in Portsmouth; and my younger brothers Struan and Ruairidh, who's an art teacher – as much as I can. The same goes for Mum and Dad. There have been times they've had to ask my siblings what country I'm in, and no one has known. I think Mum and Dad are blown away by how far I've taken things, but they can't be too surprised because they always let me roam on a long lead.

It was Mum and Dad who taught me the wonders of

wandering for wandering's sake and sleeping under the stars. They taught me that washing in rivers and pooing in fields wasn't going to kill me, that being uncomfortable – wet, cold, tired and hungry – isn't necessarily a bad thing. They allowed me to follow my dream, and I've been wandering the earth since the day I left Kilwinning. They probably think I'm a bit wild, but they're proud of me, as I'm proud of them.

Each week, I get social media messages from youngsters telling me how they've watched a programme I was in or seen a video or photo I posted and been encouraged to get off their bums and do this, that and the other. And I hope this book will do the same for you. I'm just a normal bloke. But if I can share my stories and motivate someone to change the way they live, that makes me happy. If only one person reads this book and thinks, 'I want to explore volcanoes or jungles for a living, like Aldo Kane', then brilliant. The more people who share my wonder for the world, the better. Or I hope it will encourage you to make the most of opportunities, build on what you've got, strive for things that are bigger and better and try not to look back, even when you're facing stormy waters.

I guess that's one of the main lessons I've learned on the edge: to get out there and experience things, don't miss out or put things off for another time, have fun, help people, don't be a dick, be aware of your own mortality. You don't have to do all the mad stuff I do, as long as you do something. If your head hits the pillow on a Sunday night and you're able to say, 'You know what? That was a good week, I managed to cram a lot in', you're winning at life.

Work out the kind of life you want, make a plan, and then put in the graft to get there.

There's no better way to live. Time is running out – make the most of it.

Acknowledgements

This book is a collection of the many highs and lows of my life, it touches on almost every section of my adventures, the lessons I have learned and the people who were with me at those times. Many have already been mentioned within these pages but there are a few more who need a special thank you.

Huge thanks go to writer, Ben Dirs, who had to endure many, many hours of me talking and going round in circles. Thank you for helping me to make sense of everything I have done and all I wanted to say.

I would like to thank my wife Anna and our son Atlas for putting up with my wanderings. I know it isn't always easy and you have both had the lion's share of the hard yards to deal with. I couldn't do what I do without you.

This book wouldn't have been possible if it wasn't for my management team at Mirador; Miranda Chadwick, Maddy Shipman and Jamie Slattery, and my literary agent Carly Cook at Found. All of whom have kept me focused and on the straight and narrow, especially when there were far too many other fun things to do rather than edit.

Big shout out to the whole publishing team at Yellow Kite/ Hodder & Stoughton, especially my editors Lauren Whelan and Kate Latham for all of the support and enthusiasm for my story. It's been a pleasure learning a new skill and fine tuning the process. Dan Whiteson, your illustrated maps at the beginning and end of the book are truly remarkable.

In my youth, I had a lot to be thankful for, all under the watchful guidance of my parents. Stuart & Anne Kane, thank you for the upbringing you gave me and teaching me the way of the outdoors. The Scouts (19th Ayrshire) and 1138 Ardrossan Air Cadets also hold a special place in my memories. Some of the most useful skills I have ever learned were taught to me by volunteers and those skills have served me well ever since. Of course, growing up with four siblings was one of the coolest things. Ross, Stroma, Struan & Ruairidh, I am proud to be your Bro.

The Royal Marines have played a huge part in my life since I signed the paperwork at 15 years and 9 months old. I am eternally grateful to have been part of that elite Brotherhood of Men, an exclusive Frontline club of some of the bravest, funniest, nightmarish, lovable rogues you will ever meet. Once a Marine, always a Marine PMPT.

My work has always been important to me, and I have strived to ensure that whatever I do, it's a way of life, not just a job. The Marines, Off Shore, Rope Access and finally, my ultimate passion Adventure TV. I have been in some of the most hostile, extreme and remote places on the planet working with some of the most professional people I know. Everything you see on TV usually has a producer, director, camera and sound team, researchers and fixers all working so much harder than I do. When our day is done, they are staying up all night analysing the data download, recharging batteries, sorting logistics, planning the next phases and never complaining. Here, I have found a home from home away from the Marines; small teams grafting hard in austere conditions to tight deadlines with little recognition. This is a big shout to everyone I have worked with to make those sequences amazing, without you we would literally be nothing. Special thanks to Diene Petterle who has been pushing me since we first met and had faith in my abilities. Thanks to Thursday for their continual support and banter. A special shout out to my great producer friend, master of ceremonies and general top bloke, James Woodroffe, always there in times of need with a word of ancient wisdom and a punch on the shoulder.

Finally, thank you for buying this book and spending your valuable time reading it, it's genuinely appreciated. I hope that it has added value in some way to you and inspired you to get outside, make plans and live life to the absolute best of your ability. If you have been inspired, share the love and drop the book with a friend or give it away to a random.

Big love, Aldo Kane

Picture Acknowledgements

The author and publisher would like to thank the following copyright-holders for permission to reproduce images in this book:

1. Stuart Kane
2. Royal Marines
3. Unknown photographer
4. Unknown photographer
5. Unknown photographer
6. Aldo Kane
7. Aldo Kane
8. Aldo Kane
9. Aldo Kane
10. Aldo Kane
11. Aldo Kane
12. Rob Franklin GBCT
13. Aldo Kane
14. Unknown photographer with thanks to Henry Cavill
15. Christopher Beauchamp
16. Aldo Kane with thanks to Struan Kane
17. Oliver Bailey with thanks to Jason Fox
18. Aldo Kane with thanks to Ross Johnson
19. Aldo Kane

LESSONS FROM THE EDGE

20. Unknown photographer
21. Aldo Kane
22. Keith Partridge
23. James Woodroffe/www.guymartinproper.com
24. Rob Sixsmith
25. Aldo Kane with thanks to Steve Backshall
26. Martin Hartley
27. Unknown photographer with thanks to Will Smith
28. Aldo Kane
29. Aldo Kane
30. Katy Fraser
31. Aldo Kane/Anna Williamson

About the Author

Aldo Kane is a TV adventurer, author and World Record setter with over 20 years' experience working in some of the most extreme, remote and inhospitable places on the planet. If you have watched any adventure TV in the last 10 years, then you have seen his work, either behind or in front of the camera. With almost 100 countries under his belt, there is no environment where he cannot operate. Aldo joined the Royal Marine Commandos at the age of 16 and became one of the youngest snipers in the UK armed forces. He spent 10 years operating around the globe in all environments including war in the Middle East. Leaving the Royal Marines as an expert in jungles, deserts, mountains and the Arctic, it wasn't long before Aldo started to carve a new career for himself in the TV and film industry.

Aldo now runs Vertical Planet, a technical safety risk management company providing services for some of the world's largest TV and film productions. They are often called upon to operate in some of the most extreme environments across the globe. Aldo can often be found dangling into active volcanoes, dodging cartel hitmen or squeezing underground into unknown labyrinths.